THE CONSTRUCTION ZONE

THE CONSTRUCTION ZONE

BUILDING SCAFFOLDS FOR READERS AND WRITERS

TERRY THOMPSON
Foreword by Donalyn Miller

Stenhouse
PUBLISHERS

Portland, Maine

Stenhouse Publishers
www.stenhouse.com

Some content in Part 4 previously appeared in an article by the author for ChoiceLiteracy.com called "Are You Scaffolding or Rescuing?" at www.choiceliteracy.com/articles-detail-view.php?id=735, original post date January 30, 2010.

Library of Congress Cataloging-in-Publication Data
Thompson, Terry 1970-
 The construction zone : building scaffolds for readers and writers / Terry Thompson ; foreword by Donalyn Miller.
    pages cm
 ISBN 978-1-57110-869-2 (pbk. : alk. paper) -- ISBN 978-1-62531-062-0 (ebook) 1. Reading (Elementary) 2. Creative writing (Elementary education) I. Title.
 LB1573.T496 2015
 372.4--dc23
                                                                          2015008850

Cover design, interior design, and typesetting by Alessandra S. Turati

Manufactured in the United States of America

PRINTED ON 30% PCW
RECYCLED PAPER

21 20 19 18 17 16 15   9 8 7 6 5 4 3 2 1

For Pickles

CONTENTS

FOREWORD

Back in the 1970s, before airbags and improved auto safety guidelines, small children often rode in the front seat. As the oldest, I got to ride alongside my mom in my blue booster chair. My mother was the sun in my universe, and I wanted to be as close to her as possible. As she drove, Mom shared family stories about growing up in Memphis. We sang songs with the radio such as "Let Me Be There" and "One Tin Soldier." My siblings and I chattered away, describing our days at preschool. I didn't know it at the time, but those car rides put me on the road to reading.

The first word that I read by myself was *stop*. I imagine I'm not the only one. After *stop* came *yield*, then abbreviations like *Rd.* and *Ln.* I learned to read street and business signs along our regular neighborhood routes. Next, I read labels in the grocery store. Mom and I read Richard Scarry's *Busy, Busy Town*, Dr. Seuss, and Dick and Jane together. Rereading *Go Away, Spot* one night I made the connection between a word I knew and a word in a book. *Stop* led to *Spot*. Once I understood what words could do, I never stopped reading.

Sitting in the break room at endless construction sites waiting for my electrician mother to get off work, I did my homework and flipped through discarded newspapers, picking out the words I knew and learning a few new words each time. On weekends, my mom took my younger sisters and brother and me to the public library. She let us roam into the children's section while she looked for a book of her own. As author Jess Keating says, "A kid's world is a lot bigger when they have a library to visit." I learned at an early age that books could take me almost anywhere.

Looking back, my mom says, "It was a joy to watch you learn to read. You were hungry to read." My twenty-four-year-old mother was a great first reading teacher. Through my teacher's eyes, I can see how Mom laid a strong reading foundation for my siblings and me. Talking and singing, library visits and read-alouds were foundational ingredients in a reading success recipe.

While she jokes that her kids were "born readers," Mom still struggles to read. She has trouble tracking print. She must read and reread to build meaning. Smart and driven, my mom is frustrated by the fact that reading is something she has never enjoyed. She recently told me, "I figured out when I was twenty that my reading problems held me back. I didn't want that for you kids. I didn't know anything about learning disabilities when I was growing up. I just thought I was a bad reader."

Surveying our classrooms, we see children like my mom and me (and many others)—learners with a wide range of literacy experiences and learning goals. Whether literacy comes easily to our students or they require additional support to develop strong skills, teachers must support students' progress from where they are now to where they can go next. The road from now to next isn't the same for every student, and the journey meanders more for some students than others. In spite of what we see in the movies, there are no grand epiphanies that transform teaching and learning overnight. We feed and celebrate small moments—a student who reversed her *b*s and *d*s for weeks finally cracks it, another uses text evidence in his response letter, another discovers the link between *Spot* and *stop*.

Uncovering what each child needs and providing the right instruction at the right time is challenging. Learning runs on its own schedule, and it doesn't always align with our lesson plans. There are days when we don't think anyone is learning. We worry that we are not reaching every child. We fear that we don't have the skills or mental strength to teach them all.

If we believe educational reformers and textbook publishers, teaching is too hard for teachers to figure out on their own. We receive explicit and implicit messages from people outside our profession that we are not capable of assessing our students, identifying their learning goals, or delivering effective instruction without their wisdom. Unfortunately, many of our teaching colleagues and administrators believe these messages, relying on scripted programs, test prep, computer-based intervention games, and downloadable worksheets instead of good pedagogy, kid watching, and reflective practice.

It's possible for us to be good teachers without a script. Our students need meaningful and empowering literacy experiences. Our students need relationships with more knowing others who care about them personally and believe they can learn. Teachers need these things, too. We must demand meaningful learning for ourselves and commit to career-long collaboration and professional development.

When I was a new teacher, I didn't know how to reach some of my students. I lacked experience identifying what my students needed to make progress. I could see the goal—products of learning my students had to complete, such as the book report, the essay, the end-of-year test—but I didn't know how to coach my students when their goals were all over the place.

What I needed was Terry Thompson's *Construction Zone*. With his years of teaching and coaching experience and smart advice grounded in realistic teaching challenges, Terry gives us the encouragement and tools we need to provide consistent learning for our students and invigorate our teaching. Like our students, we need scaffolding from a more knowing other who believes that we can learn and thrive. We need someone like Terry Thompson, who believes we can transform teaching and learning ourselves.

Terry begins our journey with a crisp, accessible review of the groundbreaking learning philosophies of Piaget, Vygotsky, Bruner, and Pearson and Gallagher—theorists we may not have revisited since college. Abstract ideas when introduced during our teacher education programs, concepts like social constructivism, zone of proximal development, scaffolding, and gradual release have tangible value when picturing students in our classrooms. We can call up names and faces now—students who have stretched themselves toward new learning with our support.

Naming and framing consistent conditions for instructional scaffolding—focus, flexibility, feedback, and responsibility—Terry provides teachers lenses for instruction and assessment—expanding and deepening the traditional scaffolding and gradual release model. Terry defines a progression of steps that supports teachers through a sequence of intentional lesson planning, instructional delivery, and reflection. This fluid model maintains the teacher's autonomy to select texts, design assessments, and identify individualized learning goals that match students' needs and interests.

Through relatable analogies, student examples, helpful charts, reflection questions, and a strong foundation built on learning theory and best practices, Terry Thompson's *Construction Zone* is the perfect resource for language arts teachers looking to improve their instruction so that it meets every student's learning needs. Whether you're a novice teacher or have been in the classroom for decades, *The Construction Zone* is an invaluable tool that helps calibrate our teaching toward powerful student learning and independence.

In the 1950s and '60s when my mom was a public school student, her teachers didn't know how to help her overcome her reading difficulties. As a teacher, I have struggled to help my students, too. Although there's no magic wand that transforms teaching and learning, I believe that Terry Thompson's *Construction Zone* and the professional conversations that this book will spark with colleagues can improve learning for all students and empower teachers. *The Construction Zone* will provide you with the support and advice you need to scaffold students toward independent, literate lives.

The goal of all learning is independence. We believe it for our students, and we must believe it for ourselves.

—Donalyn Miller

ACKNOWLEDGMENTS

Piglet noticed that even though he had a Very Small Heart,
it could hold a rather large amount of Gratitude.

—A. A. MILNE, *WINNIE-THE-POOH*

If you're not careful, writing a book can be a very isolating experience. It involves lots of time alone—just you, your computer, and your thoughts. You can get lost for hours searching for that perfect phrase or that just-right word until the world around you fades and you lose yourself completely in the task before you. And even when you're not hunched over your computer frantically typing away, thoughts of the writing continue to tug at you, preoccupy your thoughts, and demand your attention. In these moments, it's easy to forget that you're not alone.

But, when you finally click 'send' and return to reality, you remember that—all along—you were surrounded by friends, family, and colleagues, supporting you, encouraging you, and believing in you. And as you start to file away the piles of research that have dominated your kitchen table for months, a deep appreciation settles in and you know your work is better because of their company.

I'm fully aware that I haven't written a word of this book alone. And I'm deeply grateful for the countless others who have joined me along the way—whether through their work, their conversations, their presence, or their encouragement.

- The incredible team at Stenhouse was there the whole time, working diligently behind the scenes to bring this book to reality—especially my editor, Philippa Stratton, who waited patiently while I took the scenic route through this project, supported me when the words just wouldn't come, and kept me on track when they finally did.

- Several author friends lent a hand as well, giving valuable feedback along the way, including Jeff Anderson, Aimee Buckner, Deb Diller, Charles Fuhrken, Debbie Miller, Donalyn Miller, Mark Overmeyer, Peter Johnston—and particularly Pat Johnson and Jen Allen whose contributions improved this manuscript immensely.

- I'm grateful for the ongoing presence of Brenda Power and her website, ChoiceLiteracy.com, a valuable contribution to literacy teachers everywhere and a welcoming playground for authors like me to share new ideas and explore our thinking.

- The students, teachers, staff, and families of Windcrest Elementary in San Antonio, Texas, were with me through this process as well—all contributing to this book in ways too numerous to name here. Special thanks goes to the children there who've taught me just as much as I've taught them and the teachers who've allowed me to write about their experiences. I am also grateful for the supportive work family I've found in my instructional leadership team members—Jennifer Barton, John Merrill, Hope de Lemos, Crystal Chavez, Blythe Boeck, and Denise Holland—each of whom regularly challenge my thinking and inspire me to be a better teacher every day.

- The teachers of the original Literacy Jump Start group at River Pines Elementary were with me before this book was even an idea. Their willingness to take an open look at their instructional practices (and invite me into that process) laid the groundwork for my study of instructional rescuing and helped me explore ways to keep student responsibility aligned within our scaffolds.

- The members of the best book club ever—Jenni Clyne, Stephanie Green, Meg Grossman, Denise Holland, Nikole Jones, Holly Ledwig, Megan Marquez, and Helen White—kept me reading, thinking, and laughing throughout the entire process and offered a perfectly timed, well-needed retreat from my writing once a month.

- So many friends supported me on this journey—Angela Ford, who saw me through my perfect storm and remembered my truth when I forgot; Dwight Price and Brandon Sampson, who sent me pictures of all the fun they were having while I was at home writing; Donalyn Miller, who joined with me in redefining the term 'prewriting'; Ken McLeod, whose words of wisdom always resonate; and Jeanie Weidnebach, for being a true friend through it all.

- Of course, my parents and stepparents were there all along with their words of encouragement (Mom regularly calling to see how the writing was going) and wisdom (Dad reminding me, "You need to get off this phone and write!").

- And, my dear friend and literacy coach, Denise Holland, joined me from the start. Her love for children and the work we do, along with her incredible sense of humor, made coming to work every day a delight, while her unyielding support and excitement for this book kept me heading home to write more at the end of the day.

- Finally, Jeff, Paisley, and Carl never left my side for one moment, frequently made room in their schedules so I could write, and always reminded me—without fail—to take walks, go for a swim, and have fun. Sharing life with you is more than enough. There really are no words.

My very small heart is overflowing with gratitude for you all.

CHAPTER 1

SCAFFOLDING:
WHAT IT MEANS AND WHAT IT MEANS FOR YOU

One of the most interesting parts about writing this book has been watching everyone's reactions when I tell them what it's about. Usually it goes something like this:

"Scaffolding?"
"Yes."
"Hmm."

When that happens, I'm never quite sure what people are thinking during the brief silence that usually follows. But after they recover, a few graciously reply with something along the lines of "Oh, how exciting!" or "I look forward to reading it" before changing the subject completely. Still, some braver souls hazard a guess, following up with "Oh. You mean like . . ." and filling in the blank with their own take on scaffolding. When they do, everyone seems to have a different idea of what scaffolding is.

Even so, ask just about any teacher if he or she scaffolds learning and most will likely say they do. Probe a little more deeply, though, and we might start to diverge on the finer details of our understandings of the scaffolding process. Some may sincerely answer that they thought they did, but now that you ask, they aren't so sure. It seems that when most of us are pressed for clear details around the concept, things start to go in a confusing labyrinth of different directions.

Though many of us understand scaffolding as a way to support learning, our attempts to go deeper often leave us pensive. Faces scrunched up. Lips pursed. Convinced we do in fact know what it is, but struggling to word it concisely. And if we're having a hard time defining it, imagine how difficult it might be to have professional conversations around it—let alone actually do it. Despite these complexities, *scaffolding* remains one of those perennial terms that has wound its way seamlessly into our collective psyche.

Part of what makes scaffolding so tough to pin down is that it's essentially based in a metaphor—the idea of supporting students as they build independence—and metaphors leave lots of room for interpretation. On one hand, this versatility is helpful because it allows us to tailor the image in a variety of ways to fit our needs and growing understanding of the process. But these same benefits can also have the opposite effect, making scaffolding difficult to puzzle out definitively.

It makes sense, then, that teachers might have varying ideas of what scaffolding is.

With that in mind, this book aims to explore scaffolding by honoring its broad complexities while starting small. Together, we'll explore this multifaceted concept from a specific angle where scaffolded instruction characterizes a pattern of teaching that shifts the level of responsibility for the learning from the *more knowing other* (you!) to the *less knowing other* (your student). We'll expand on that idea as we work from a common definition that centers on five fundamental factors:

1. a ***more knowing other*** supporting

2. a ***novice*** in reaching

3. some sort of educational ***outcome*** the learner could not yet reach alone

4. in a ***constructive*** way

5. that is ***temporary***, steadily fading as the novice gets closer to (and eventually reaches) the intended outcome.

These factors seem straightforward at first, but when you take a moment to consider them more deeply, you'll soon arrive at the thought that there's got to be a whole lot more to it. For a more expansive view, we'll need to move beyond this basic description and look at the principles that form the bedrock of scaffolding.

LEARNING HOW WE LEARN: THE RESEARCH BEHIND SCAFFOLDING

The way we learn is a very intricate, personal experience. Thankfully, students come to us each school year with an innate ability and desire to learn.

JEAN PIAGET: CONSTRUCTION OF UNDERSTANDING

Swiss psychologist Jean Piaget taught us that our students are hardwired—as all humans are—to take in new information and experiences and incorporate them into their constantly evolving schemas. His theory of learning holds that, much like a pre-K student who independently figures out her iPad camera function, children gain knowledge through increasingly complex mental activities and interactions with their environment. To put it another way, children *construct* their own understandings as they take on new knowledge, adding to what they already know by trial and error, keeping what works and tossing out what doesn't, until they arrive at an entirely new level of understanding. Piaget's theory, also known as **constructivism**, reminds us that, whether we're teaching them or not, children are in a constant state of active learning. In essence, the students in our classrooms aren't sitting by passively, waiting for us. They are *active* participants in the learning process (Mercer and Hodgkinson 2008; Ginsberg and Opper 1988).

But humans are also social animals. Along with that instinctive drive to learn is an equally powerful need to establish and build relationships with others. We need to interact with others in a meaningful way—others who empower us in our evolution to become more than we were before. Others who help us grow spiritually, emotionally, and intellectually.

This is where you come in.

LEV VYGOTSKY: THE ZONE OF PROXIMAL DEVELOPMENT

Lev Vygotsky, a Russian psychologist working around the same time as Piaget, would argue that you're one of these "others"—an integral part of a delicate learning process along with millions of others just like you. In fact, you're what Vygotsky might call a *more knowing other*.

Central to Vygotsky's theory is the idea that, through social interactions with this more knowledgeable person, learners are able to progress from what they are able to understand alone to knowledge that is just beyond their grasp. In this way, the construction of knowledge is a *social* endeavor—so we refer to Vygotsky's work as **social constructivism** (Mercer and Hodgkinson 2008). Vygotsky called the space between the learner's current level of achievement and that next level of knowledge she can't accomplish alone the **zone of proximal development (ZPD)**. Vygotsky (1978) believed that through interactive conversations, the more knowing other guides the child through a series of learning experiences that continually unfurl as the zone of proximal development expands with each successive experience (see Figure 1.1). In effect, our instruction is most successful when we're teaching in that just-right place that rests squarely between what students can already do and what they can't do alone. When you reflect on your own teaching, you'll probably notice that outside of this zone, instruction falters and loses its way.

For instance, if we continually teach what our children already control (the zone of *actual* development), we've made the learning too easy and run the risk of losing them to boredom. If, on the other hand, the majority of our instruction occurs in areas they aren't quite ready for (the zone of *potential* development), we've made the learning too difficult and could easily lose them to frustration and resistance. When we work in the zone of proximal development, opportunities are ripe to support our students in just the right way—challenging, helping, and adjusting to higher or lower levels of support while guiding them across the zone of proximal development.

Vygotsky (1986) upped the ante on Piaget's thinking with the idea that, although children are certainly active participants in the construction of knowledge, a more knowing other facilitates this learning through social interactions and conversation. In this *construction zone* of sorts, the teacher and student are essentially constructing knowledge together. In fact, it is in this concept of a more knowing other supporting a learner through the zone of proximal development that scaffolding finds its structure.

JEROME BRUNER: SCAFFOLDING

American psychologist Jerome Bruner and his colleagues first introduced us to the metaphor of *scaffolding* as a useful way to conceptualize what Vygotsky meant by the zone of proximal development (Wood, Bruner, and Ross 1976). Here, in much the same way as a physical scaffold supports a builder until he is able to complete his work, scaffolding is the path a teacher charts to guide

ZONE OF ACTUAL DEVELOPMENT	ZONE OF PROXIMAL DEVELOPMENT	ZONE OF POTENTIAL DEVELOPMENT
What the learner can actually do without support or assistance	What the learner can do with the support of a more knowing other as he moves from one level of understanding to the next	What the learner could potentially do alone after passing through the zone of proximal development

Figure 1.1
Diagram of the Zone of Proximal Development

learners from point A, the zone of *actual* development, to point B, the zone of *potential* development (see Figure 1.2).

Instructional scaffolding, then, is a thoughtful course through Vygotsky's zone of proximal development that includes a series of actionable steps, decisions, and interactions that support the learner in growing toward increasing degrees of independence. It differentiates itself from other ways learning might occur, because students are actively involved in a rich, interactive experience that invites them to construct new learning with a teacher who supports them every step of the way, offering just enough assistance while allowing them to take on greater stages of independence the instant they're ready.

ZONE OF ACTUAL DEVELOPMENT	ZONE OF PROXIMAL DEVELOPMENT	ZONE OF POTENTIAL DEVELOPMENT
What the learner can actually do without support or assistance	What the learner can do with the support of a more knowing other as he moves from one level of understanding to the next	What the learner could potentially do alone after passing through the zone of proximal development
Too Easy	Just Right	Too Hard
Disinterest	Motivation	Frustration
Point A ➝	Scaffolding ➝	Point B

Figure 1.2
Expanded Diagram of Zone of Proximal Development

This marriage of thinking from prominent scholars such as Vygotsky, Piaget, and Bruner helps us understand the philosophical groundings of scaffolding, but up to this point, the concept might still seem too theoretical and elusive, giving rise to still more questions. For instance, how exactly do we do that? How do we clearly plot courses across the zone of proximal development every day in real classrooms? How do we release learners to increasing degrees of independence? And, what would that even look like?

PEARSON AND GALLAGHER: THE GRADUAL RELEASE OF RESPONSIBILITY

Pearson and Gallagher (1983) offered solutions to these questions in a framework known as the gradual release of responsibility model. As a way to operationalize Vygotsky and Bruner's work, the gradual release of responsibility model gives us a user-friendly structure for how, over time, the teacher moves from a highly supportive role to that of a less involved participant as the learner increasingly takes on greater responsibility for the work. Currently one of the best-known modes of instruction, the gradual release progression is most recognized in its three stages of successful instruction (see Figure 1.3) that shift from modeling to guided practice to independence:

- *Modeling:* (I do) where the teacher models while explaining the goal for the learner

- *Guided Practice:* (We do) where the teacher works with the student, gradually pulling back the level of support as the student gains independence

- *Independence:* (You do) where the teacher pulls back completely and the student works independently

For example, when my friend Iris decided it would be fun to teach me how to knit, she first talked me through the process—"Loop, around, pull off, tighten"—while I watched her do it (*modeling*). After several minutes of my just watching, she put the needles into my hands and then reached over and put her hands right on top of mine. As she guided my hands with hers, she continued to repeat, "Loop, around, pull off, tighten" (*guided practice*). Eventually, she pulled her hands away, continuing to chant, "Loop, around, pull off, tighten," jumping back in when I lost my way (*guided practice*). Before long, she just sat back and watched me as I took over, repeating to myself while knitting, "Loop, around, pull off, tighten" (*independence*).

TEACHER RESPONSIBILITY		STUDENT RESPONSIBILITY
Modeling (I do)	Guided Practice (We do)	Independent Practice (You do)

Figure 1.3
Common Interpretation of the Gradual Release of Responsibility Model

This three-stage structure of the gradual release of responsibility model shapes the skeleton of a variety of similar learning frameworks (see Figure 1.4), so it's probably sounding familiar to you. How you label the stages of the gradual release pattern seems to be a matter of personal (and sometimes, philosophical) preference, but because it so clearly exemplifies how a more knowing other might bring a learner through the zone of proximal development, the gradual release of responsibility model has become, for many teachers, synonymous with scaffolding.

Is the classic diagram in Figure 1.3 too simplistic? Probably. But keep in mind, it was never meant to encompass all that scaffolding is or can be. Rather, it was meant to give us a basic grasp of scaffolding. For a more

TEACHER RESPONSIBILITY			STUDENT RESPONSIBILITY
I do	We do		You do
I go	We go		You go
Modeled	Guided Practice		Independent Practice
I do/You watch	I do/You help	You do/I help	You do/I watch
I do it	We do it	You do it together	You do it alone

Figure 1.4
Variations of the Gradual Release Model

detailed understanding, we have to look more closely at what goes on inside this innocent little rectangle.

SCAFFOLDING: FOUR COMMON CONDITIONS

Beyond its basic diagram, scaffolding is an incredibly complicated process that would take volumes of books to explore definitively, and certainly no one diagram could ever make scaffolding easy. There are as many routes to independence as there are children in our classrooms, and no book could tell you everything you need to know about instructional scaffolding or what to do in every situation with every student and every goal. With this in mind, remember that this book isn't aiming for a global, comprehensive analysis of scaffolding. For instance, we're not going to discuss symmetrical scaffolding, in which collaborative groups scaffold themselves to independence, nor will we cover other supportive processes such as whole-to-part learning and invitational learning that are just as effective. Since scaffolding can manifest itself in a variety of ways, we'll keep things manageable by concentrating our attention solely on those scaffolding structures in the traditional educational setting that involve the teacher as the more knowing other supporting learners in that just-right zone of proximal development.

We'll further fine-tune our focus by considering the role we play in this process while directing our lens at four common conditions that apply to any scaffolding scenario, regardless of group size, educational setting, content area, instructional goal, delivery method, how it's characterized, or even the learners involved. These four common conditions are *focus, flexibility, feedback,* and *responsibility.*

1. **Focus**: Based in recursive and ongoing assessment paired with an understanding of the learner, we are proactive, teaching toward a clear, deliberate goal.

2. **Flexibility**: Tethered to our focus, our scaffolds have a responsive, organic quality and shift with perfect timing to meet the specific needs of our learners.

3. **Feedback**: Strong scaffolds exist and expand in an ongoing feedback loop that emphasizes and builds on students' thinking so they can monitor how they're doing and take the next, right steps toward independence.

4. **Responsibility**: Our motivation in every scaffolding scenario is to place optimal levels of responsibility on the learner at every step in the process, so that our students are eventually independently responsible for the new knowledge.

As we move forward, we'll repeatedly highlight the fact that our scaffolds are strongest when we deliberately consider the influence of our work while practicing *intentionality* and *reflection* around these four common conditions (Figure 1.5). With this in mind, the chapters that follow are divided into four parts, each focusing on one condition, so you can take an introspective look at the principle itself, your instructional practices around it, and how you can capitalize on it to improve your scaffolds.

But make no mistake: scaffolding is a shared endeavor. Remember, this is the construction zone. This is where you and your students work together to construct new learning. Even though we'll be looking more specifically at our role in this process, know that we are doing so primarily in an effort to explore how our instruction can most effectively support this shared load and the incremental process of releasing its full responsibility to our learners.

Figure 1.5
Scaffolding with Intentionality and Reflection

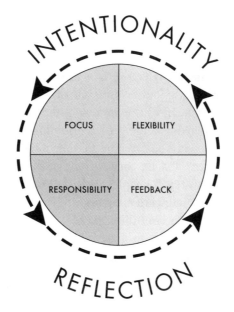

Teaching involves more variables than many of us have ever really had the time or inclination to investigate. What's more, the majority of those qualities stand completely outside of our control. We have little or no power over the mandated curricula we're expected to cover, the overwhelming workload we carry, the insufficient time lines we're expected to work within, the abilities of the students we're given, or the parenting they get at home. Nor are we able to manage the learning that occurred in previous grade levels, the out-of-date materials we're frequently given to teach with, the ineffective programs we're often expected to maintain, or even the high-stakes testing our students have to sit through year after year.

Variables like these—these roadblocks to our work—can sometimes paralyze us, leaving us feeling powerless and questioning our ability to effect real change. But the reality is that we can change only what we can control. We can suggest. We can influence. We can empower. But we can't change.

The only thing you have any control over—the only thing you can really change—is yourself.

Although this book is certainly about scaffolding, it's just as much about the role *you* play in that process. Together, we'll look at curriculum goals, student needs, and several familiar tenets of education. But we'll depart slightly from traditional explorations of these subjects as I invite you to spend some time reflecting on yourself, your instructional decisions, and the effect of your actions on the children learning in your classroom every day.

As you read, I encourage you to think about your own practices and how they relate to the discussions. If you're new to scaffolding, let this book be a starting place of a career-long journey into one of the most effective ways you can support your students. If you're revisiting the concept, take some time to reflect on how your understanding of scaffolding has changed since you first learned about it, where you are now in your interpretation, and how the material in this book can enhance your current work with young readers and writers. To help with this, each chapter ends with questions designed to get you thinking and move you toward applying its principles in your own work.

This may be harder than you think. Like nurses, therapists, counselors, and other types of caretakers, teachers are helpers by nature. Our lives revolve around other people's needs, so spending time reflecting on ourselves can feel unnatural and maybe even a bit selfish. Scaffolding involves the decisive, actionable steps we take during the learning process, and this requires a certain mindfulness on our part. Our teaching decisions are stronger when we're acting within our awareness rather than outside of it. We have to find ways to move our thoughts and decision-making process to the conscious level. Effective instructional scaffolds require teachers who are *reflective* about their role in the scaffolding process and are *intentional* about their movements within it.

If we truly want to make a difference, then we start by looking at our instruction differently. If you've been working with the mind-set of "Once I know everything I need to know, *then* I can be the teacher I set out to be in the beginning," realize that it doesn't work that way.

Teaching consciously is a practice—moment by moment, day by day. Just like our students, we learn from our successes and our failures. Learning to craft effective scaffolds is an ongoing practice that starts *now* and grows from here. *This* is where we begin—teaching with intentionality and reflection, in full awareness of what we're doing and why.

Welcome to the construction zone!

CONSTRUCTIVE REFLECTIONS

1. How do you define scaffolding? Do you struggle to come up with a clear definition for it? Would your peers define it the same way? How does your definition compare with the information presented in this chapter?

2. How do you see the relationship between scaffolding and the gradual release progression? Are they the same thing? Different? Would your colleagues agree?

Aside from the stressors of our work, many things can keep us from being self-reflective. Using this list, take an honest inventory of any barriers that might block your ability to be reflective.

- Discomfort – Like most helpers, you may have trained yourself to focus more on others, so self-reflection instinctively may make you feel uneasy.

- Uncertainty – It may be the case that you don't have a process for self-reflection, or maybe you just aren't sure what to look for when you do sit down to reflect.

- Effort – Self-reflection requires time and energy, two things most of us lack. As with other things, such as exercise or grocery shopping, sometimes it's just easier not to do it.

- Unaware – You may have never realized how important self-reflection is, so it's just not part of your regular process yet.

- Fear – Looking at ourselves honestly can make us nervous because we may not like what we see.

- Obligation –You may avoid self-reflection because you worry that what you find will likely prompt some sort of movement toward change, and you're simply not ready to commit to that.

3. Think about a lesson you've taught well. How aligned were you with the learners' zone of proximal development in that situation? What about a lesson that didn't go so well?

4. As an instructor, how do you know when you've made it through the zone of proximal development? How do you monitor for this?

5. This chapter closes with a recommendation to teach with intentionality and reflection. How self-reflective are you about your work with learners? What are your current practices around this? In what ways could you be more mindful about your work with readers and writers? And, what effects might improving these practices have?

PART ONE

FOCUS

Based in recursive and ongoing assessment paired with an understanding of the learner, we are proactive, teaching toward a clear, deliberate goal.

CHAPTER 2   GETTING FOCUSED:
IDENTIFYING
LEARNING TARGETS

I'm not a very athletic person. So it won't surprise you that, each spring during middle school, I looked forward to my favorite P.E. unit: archery. Anytime I could avoid breaking a sweat, I was pleased.

Comfortable in that air-conditioned gym, I'd draw back my bow and carelessly point somewhere in the vicinity of the target. I didn't have a clue what I was doing. I defined my success in archery by just hitting the target. Anywhere on the target was fine by me. Sometimes, by surprise, I'd actually hit the bull's-eye. But if that happened at all—and that's a big *if*—it had nothing to do with any premeditated strategy on my part.

My two brothers enjoyed archery as well, but they were far more competitive. In fact, they were driven. While I sat in the library reading *Where the Red Fern Grows* for the third time, they were off sharpening their skills with clear, deliberate focus. They bought professional-grade bows and signed up at the local archery range for additional practice. When they shot arrows, I was always amazed at how often they'd hit the bull's-eye—which they seemed to do with calculated precision.

Of course, they were so much better than I was because they practiced. They were considerably more invested in hitting the bull's-eye than I was, so they spent their energies on what was most important to that end: improving their aim.

When we plan our scaffolds for readers and writers, it's not enough to land somewhere on the target. Every time we draw back our instructional arrow and release it, it should fly straight and steady, landing solidly in the center of the bull's-eye of the learning goal. With this in mind, we turn our attention to the first of scaffolding's four common conditions:

> *Grounded in assessment, a clear, intentional focus is the driving force behind any scaffolding scenario.*

One of the conscious teacher's main priorities in the construction zone is to clearly articulate the instructional goal—first for ourselves and then for our students. Without a fine-tuned focus, our scaffolds fall apart before we can even get started, and we miss the bull's-eye entirely.

There is power in specificity.

PRACTICING OUR PRECISION: RELEVANT VERSUS RELATED INSTRUCTION

The effectiveness of our scaffold is directly related to the clarity of our focus. But too often, what keeps us from moving our learners forward is the lack of clear vision on our part—we can't see where we're going. And when what we're doing in the present isn't connected to a clear vision, we're left feeling depleted, frustrated, and ineffective.

This happens all the time. Consider how you learned to ride a bicycle. More than likely, you started out with training wheels and, after getting your bearings, blissfully rode along with them for some time. Then eventually someone—who *seemed* to know what they were doing—removed your training wheels, saying you were ready to ride a big-kid bike without them.

Reluctant, but trusting that you were, indeed, ready, you pushed off the pedal with one foot, ready to face the world without training wheels.

And then you fell.

People commonly use training wheels as an analogy for scaffolding. In truth, according to bike experts (Day 2012) they're actually a great example of an unclear focus within a scaffold. You see, the reason you fell was that that smarter person who you trusted to teach you to ride a bike was trying to use training wheels to teach you to *balance*. Training wheels may teach you to *pedal* and *steer*, but they don't teach you to balance. To be fair, your big person probably wasn't aware of the mismatch. Parents have used training wheels for ages, so it made sense at the time.

Here's the rub. If the instructional goal is to teach a novice rider to balance while riding, a much better option would be to remove the pedals and lower the seat so that he can touch the ground. In this way, he can develop his sense of balance by repeatedly pushing off with his feet and sailing forward, initially in small spurts but eventually in longer strides. Once his balance is developed, you can raise the seat, reinstall the pedals, and teach him to ride a real bike with ease.

This mismatch between a teaching decision and its goal illustrates the classic difference between *relevant* instruction and *related* instruction. When our aim is clearly focused on the bull's-eye, we can say that what we're doing is relevant to our goal. But often, we find that our instruction, though possibly *related* to what we're trying to accomplish, isn't directly *relevant*. In this case, training wheels are related to the broader goal of teaching a child to ride a bike, because we might use them to teach him to pedal and steer, but not directly relevant to balancing—our actual, intended goal. When it's all said and done, our arrow ends up somewhere in the vicinity of the target but not directly on the bull's-eye, leaving the teacher and learner frustrated—if not a bit bandaged and bruised.

We see evidence of this pattern in our teaching, too. Curious about a discussion I'd led at a recent staff meeting on this issue, Lauren called me down to her room to offer a second opinion on some of her instructional decisions. From her running records, Lauren had noticed that about five readers from her second-grade class were consistently struggling with a similar error pattern. With all of their running records laid out across her small-group table, she pointed out how the majority of each student's errors showed meaningful mistakes that looked similar to the word they were attempting to read. For instance, all five of them read *quickly* for *quietly* in the sentence "The mouse quietly darted across the kitchen floor." This error pattern continued with other misreads such as *liked* for *loved*, *scurrying* for *scampering*, and *those* for *these*.

"Okay," I said after she'd finished. "In light of this, what've you decided? Where will you go next with these readers?"

"Well, it's great that they're trying to make sense in the story, but they're not paying attention to the middle parts of words. I definitely want to add a larger word work part to their small-group lesson, and I came up with this activity, but now I'm worried that it might be more related than relevant."

The activity she handed over was a traditional cloze passage—a paragraph with several missing words for the readers to fill in. In each blank, she'd put the first letter of the missing word. In effect, the students would need to think about a word that started with the first letter and, at the same time, made sense in the paragraph. During the discussion, Lauren shared that her intention with this activity was to support the readers in thinking about the middles of words.

It turned out that Lauren's suspicions were right. This activity—though related to her instructional goal of attending to middle sounds—wasn't directly relevant to what she was trying to get her readers to do. Sure, they'd be writing middle (and ending) sounds for the words that would fill in the blank. But the error patterns she'd originally noticed in their running records showed us that these readers were already experts at filling in a word that made sense and started with the correct sound. In fact, that was part of the problem.

After some thought, we decided each of the groups' lessons would include a word study activity that was directly relevant to helping these five readers attend to differences in middle sounds. To be more specific, Lauren would craft word ladders where the first and last sound of all the words on the ladder stayed the same and only the middles changed. In addition to this regular activity, Lauren decided that she would look for opportunities to highlight the error pattern with students individually by writing their error attempt and the correct word (one on top of the other) on the whiteboard and having the readers circle the parts of the two words that were different (Figure 2.1). As she did this, she continued to affirm their cuing strengths by prompting them to cross-check their efforts against whether or not each made sense and sounded right.

Figure 2.1a
A student in the group looks for the differences between her attempts and the words in the text.

Figure 2.1b
Word ladders help Lauren's students focus on the middles of words.

In this instance, Lauren made a critical instructional shift by reflecting on her work alongside the needs of her students. She brought her aim into focus. When we raise our planning to this conscious level, we're able to make clear, informed decisions about exactly where we want to take our learners. Our aim must be calculated and precise. Once it is, we can tether the other scaffolding conditions—*flexibility*, *feedback,* and *responsibility*—to that aim.

Our instructional arrow heads directly for the bull's-eye.

A strong, maintained focus is the constant thread woven through the sequence of an effective scaffolding process. Without it, the scaffold itself ceases to exist. But it can be difficult to wade through the variety of student needs and an escalating list of other diversions to find the right place to start and then figure out which way to go. And trying to stay focused can sometimes leave you feeling like you're playing a frantic game of instructional *Where's Waldo?*

Focus is *holding the goal in sight despite all other distractions*. This definition underscores two main qualities: establishing a goal and maintaining our direction toward it. To this end, the remainder of this chapter is structured around *getting focused.* In the following chapter we'll consider the challenge of *staying focused.*

GETTING FOCUSED

I grew up in a small town and couldn't wait to move to the big city. As soon as I finished college, I made a beeline to the nearest metropolitan area: Houston, Texas. When I look back on it all, I'm still not sure what I was thinking. Houston is the fourth-largest city in the United States, and finding my way in that kind of traffic was something I was completely unprepared for. Navigating a ten-lane highway with all the other drivers zipping by at warp speed past multiple exchanges, oddly marked exits, and endless loops, I felt real fear for the first time.

Since I was determined to avoid moving back home, and GPS systems weren't yet available, I had to figure out how to drive in my new city. With that in mind, I decided I needed to get to know Houston a little better. Really get to know it. So, a few nights a week, I'd set my alarm for 2:30 in the morning, get in my car, and drive. Just drive. Without the constraints of traffic, I was able to wander all over the city. If I had somewhere particular I'd be driving to in the next few days, I'd make sure to explore that route during one of my middle-of-the-night drives. But mostly, I just drove to get used to where everything was and how the Houston road system worked.

Before long, I got to know the ins and outs of the city and its layout. I was able to drive in its traffic much more easily and, in no time at all, became a real Houston driver. (If you've driven in Houston, you know exactly what that means.) Anyone who's ever tried to drive in an unfamiliar city can attest to this. It's easier when you know what you're dealing with.

Plotting a course through our scaffolds can be similarly challenging. Most of us can find the target—or at least land on it somewhere—but it's the fine-tuning for the bull's-eye that can be difficult. Luckily, like all teachers, you have an instructional GPS that can guide you through the zone of proximal development in the same way your car's GPS gets you to your destination—by asking three important questions:

- Where are we going?

- Where are we right now?

- What's the best way to get there? (See Chapter 3.)

WHERE ARE WE GOING? THINKING LIKE A GPS

Although this may seem like a simple question, it requires some reflection. In fact it's critical. If we don't know where we're going, we'll never get there. As Rick Stiggins reminds us, "Students can hit any education target they can see that holds still for them" (Stiggins et al. 2004, 57). Just as when we're using a real GPS, a clear understanding of where we're headed lays the foundation for our route. The more exact the address we enter, the more likely we are to arrive at our destination.

Thinking proactively, we get clear about our destination by homing in on two important characteristics found in any effective learning goal:

- a specific action

- tied to an explicit outcome.

These two central components can make or break a learning objective, and being clear about them can be the difference between teaching that is directly relevant and teaching that is coincidentally related. When we begin with a goal that's too vague, our instruction tends to veer off course. For instance, take a look at the following learning goals:

*Learning Goal One—Marcus will read a text
level C.*

*Learning Goal Two—Marcus will cross-check
meaning from picture support with first-letter visual
cues to read a text level C.*

Which learning goal is more specific? Both denote an explicit outcome—
to read at a text level C. But Learning Goal One isn't clear about the action
the learner needs to take for that to happen. The only action it mentions is that
Marcus will *read*, which perhaps points us in the right direction but is open to
wide interpretation. It isn't specific enough. Learning Goal Two, on the other
hand, tells us exactly what we'd need to observe Marcus doing once he takes
responsibility for the goal—*cross-checking his meaningful attempts with the
first letter of the word he's reading*. With this clarity, we know precisely what
we're aiming for. We can enter an exact address in our instructional GPS. The
more explicit we can be about the action and the outcome within our learning
objectives, the stronger our teaching becomes (see Figure 2.2).

Be especially diligent around goals that you didn't generate. Off-track
planning can certainly happen when you haven't crafted a learning goal clearly
enough for yourself, but it can also occur in the confusion that results from trying

GOAL *UNCLEAR ADDRESS*	GOAL *EXACT ADDRESS*
read a text level C	crosscheck picture meaning with initial visual cues to read a text level C
write with better word choice	identify and use similes and descriptive nouns as craft techniques writers use to create visual images
create mental images to support stronger comprehension	visualize characters' facial expressions and actions to infer their feelings and motivation
read fluently	use punctuation to read with appropriate phrasing and inflection
understand poetry	analyze figurative language to infer meaning in poetry

Figure 2.2
When we program learning goals into our instructional GPS, we must be clear about where we're going,
tying a specific action to an explicit outcome.

After deciding where you're going by defining the goal's action and outcome, you might further fine-tune your focus by asking some clarifying follow-up questions to gather more information:

- **Whose goal is it?** Essentially an origin question, we ask ourselves, "Where did this come from?" Some goals are dictated to us directly (curricular goals), whereas others identify themselves as we're working with learners (customized goals) and are based on student need and progress. Being aware of this can help us understand the goal at a deeper level.

- **What other goals coordinate with this one?** Often, instructional objectives are integrated with several other goals at the same time and frequently serve as stair steps to even higher, more involved targets. Still other goals might occur alongside each other simultaneously. Knowing where a learning objective falls in the grand scheme of things can shed some light on its purpose and make it clearer.

(Continued on next page.)

to decipher a state- or nationally dictated curricular objective that's often wordier than the Constitution. In either case, drill down to those two pillars—find the *specific action* and its *explicit outcome*—and your goal will start to become clearer.

MIRACLE QUESTION

To further clarify your focus, it may help to ask yourself, "What would my students need to be doing to reach this learning goal? More specifically, what would it look like, what would it sound like, and what would be happening as a result of that action?" A method you might use to this end is called the Miracle Question.

The Miracle Question definitely requires some imagination on your part, but it can help you pinpoint exactly what it is you want your learners to accomplish. Essentially, you imagine that you had to take the day off and that while you were gone, your substitute worked a miracle and scaffolded your students to the identified goal for you. When you return, you find your students successfully performing the learning objective. If all this actually happened, the Miracle Question asks, what's the *first thing* you would notice? More often than not, naming the first thing you would notice steers you to the specific action your goal will be built around, and with this renewed clarity, you can plan better instruction toward it.

If we used this technique for Marcus (mentioned above), whose goal was to cross-check meaning from picture support with first-letter visual cues to read a text level C, one of the first things I would notice is that his eyes are moving from the pictures to the words, and the words he reads make sense and start with the correct sound. Looking at Marcus's goal through the lens of the Miracle Question zeros in on the specific action and explicit outcome mentioned earlier. You can deepen the Miracle Question (and your focus) by asking yourself further questions such as these: "If I entered the room wearing earplugs and couldn't hear a thing, what's the first thing I would *see*? If I were blindfolded, what's the first thing I would *hear*?"

FOCUS PHRASE

Another practical technique you can use while getting focused is called a *focus phrase*. A focus phrase is a short, student-friendly statement of the goal that you and the learner repeat throughout the scaffolding process. For instance, Marcus's focus phrase might be this one:

> *"My words match the picture and start with the right sound."*

Since the phrase is repeated frequently, its language keeps the instruction and learning anchored to the goal throughout the lesson. The focus phrase is beneficial in three significant ways:

1. It keeps the teacher focused on the goal during planning and delivery.

2. It keeps the student focused on the goal throughout the instruction.

3. It becomes the source for students' self-talk when working independently, which eventually becomes part of their inner thoughts.

A focus phrase requires us to narrow the learning goal to its fundamental details and then to look at those details through our students' eyes. Because of this, the process of crafting the wording for a focus phrase concentrates our thoughts and planning on exactly what we're trying to accomplish and exactly what our learners will need to do. With this clarified understanding, we can move with greater precision toward the goal.

(Continued from page 22.)

- **What pitfalls surround this goal?** What is this objective like or unlike? What are some possible related (but not relevant) instructional moves that might veer us away from the target? Taking some time to explore what a goal is not helps us clarify what it actually is.

- **How will you know when you've met this goal?** Clear goals are measurable. You can tell when you've reached them. Knowing the specific performance standards for a learning objective before you start can help refine your focus. Some teachers I've worked with find it valuable to ask, "How will this be assessed?"

As you plan your focus phrases, be sure they're practical. In his book *How the Brain Learns* David Sousa (2011) reminds us, "Keep the number of items in a lesson objective within the capacity limits of students, and they are likely to remember more of what they learned. Less is more!" (51). When you set out to devise a focus phrase, remember that a strong focus phrase is

- concise and manageable,

- written in student-friendly language,

- based in a clearly defined goal, and

- maintains the integrity of the focus throughout the scaffold.

Once you've prepared your focus phrase, you can put it to work as a verbally repeated thread woven throughout your scaffold. You repeat it in your mind as you're planning to keep your instruction intentional, you repeat it with your students as you work together to keep you both focused, and over time, your students take on its language, repeating it to themselves unconsciously and independently.

To further illustrate this concept, let's return to Lauren's second graders. Recall, these readers were making meaningful attempts that started and ended with the correct sounds but were jumbled up in the middle. Together, Lauren and I crafted a focus phrase to support these readers in attending to sounds all the way across words:

"I run the bases across words as I read."

This simple language drew on the analogy that when a batter runs the bases, he has to go in the right direction quickly, touching each base in order. As Lauren and I settled in for the group's next guided reading lesson, I introduced the focus phrase:

TT:
Guys, have you ever played baseball or softball?

S1:
Yes!

S2:
I haven't, but I watch it on TV.

S3:

I've never played that . . .

TT:

Well, have you played kickball before? I think I've seen you play that.

S3:

Oh, yeah . . . I've done that. Are we going to play kickball?

TT:

Well, sort of. We're going to *run the bases across our words* when we read. I've been listening in while all of you read, and I've noticed something I think I can help you out with. Take a look at this word [*writes the word* these *on the whiteboard*]. Yesterday when it was time to read, each one of you got to this word and said this word instead [*writes the word* those *right on top of the word* these] . . .

S4:

That's wrong!

S2:

Yeah. That one's *these* and that one is *those*!

TT:

Yeah, I know . . . they're really close though and they both sort of make sense. It's an easy mistake.

S3:

Yeah . . . they're almost the same.

S1:

Almost.

TT:

Yeah . . . almost. How are they different?

S4:

[*points to the middles*] That one has an *o* and . . . the other one . . . it has an *e*!

TT:

You're right . . . it does. See, that's what I wanted to talk to you about. You know how as soon as you hit the baseball or kick the kickball, you take off running?

All:

Yeah!

TT:

And you run quickly around the bases in order? And you touch each base along the way? And you run all the way home?

[*All nod.*]

TT:

What happens if you forget to touch a base and you keep running?

S3:

You're out . . . it doesn't count!

TT:

Yeah! You have to touch them all or it doesn't count. You have to *run the bases*. It's the same way when you read words. You have to go in order, touching each part of the words with your eyes and making sure what you say matches. You *run the bases across words when you read*. Everybody say that, *"I run the bases across words when I read!"*

All:

I run the bases across words when I read!

TT:

Yeah. That's it! Let me show you what I mean . . . look here at the words *those* and *these* . . . if you got to the word *these* and read *those* instead – you missed a base with your eyes. You touched first base [*points to* th], skipped second, and then ran all the way home [*points to* s *and* e]! If you don't touch all the bases with your eyes, it doesn't count.

S3:

Yeah. It doesn't count . . .

TT:

Watch me *run the bases* across this word while I read it . . . [*continues to model*]

As you review this exchange, notice how frequently some form of the focus phrase comes up. This is intentional. The main goal for the focus phrase is that after hearing it and repeating it frequently, the concept eventually becomes second nature for the student—taking advantage of the concept that the learner eventually internalizes the language shared during interactions with the more knowing other (Vygotsky 1978; Berk and Winsler 1995). The more the focus phrase is repeated, the stronger the focus becomes and the more likely learners are to take on the language for themselves and, over time, incorporate it into their thinking.

As the group moved from modeling to shared support and eventually to independence, Lauren and I were on constant lookout for authentic moments where we could prompt, reinforce, or give reminders for students to *run the bases across words* while they were reading. Within a handful of lessons, all but one reader was finding success attending to sounds across words.

Focus phrases can be crafted for individual, small-group, or whole-group goals and can support every stage of the learning process. I find this method such a valuable tool for keeping me and my learners on track instructionally that I often write focus phrases at the top of my lesson plan or near the individual student's name on my conferring clipboard. Having it right there where I can see it reminds me of my focus and keeps me on track throughout the scaffolding process (see Figure 2.3).

WHERE ARE WE RIGHT NOW?
STARTING WITH ASSESSMENT

After you enter the exact address in your car's GPS, the next question it asks is "Where are we right now?" It's a critical question. Having a destination isn't enough. To plot a direct course your GPS needs to know where you're starting out. Strong instructional scaffolding depends on a similar dichotomy. Once we have our instructional objective clearly defined, we have to figure out exactly where our learners are in relation to that goal before we can plot the best course. And, as always, the more precise we can be, the better.

Imagine you rush to the doctor's office doubled over with severe abdominal pain, and without so much as a hello, your doctor writes out a prescription, hands it to you, and walks out of the room. Likely, you'd make a mad dash for

GOAL	FOCUS PHRASE
search for and use meaning to support word solving	I think about the picture and get my mouth ready for the first sound.
reading with phrasing	As I read, I group words that go together.
attending to elements of fiction	When I read fiction, I pay attention to the characters, setting, and plot.
visualizing text	I make a movie in my mind as I read.
correcting overuse of uppercase letters	I use capitals only when I need them.
predicting	When I read, I think about the text and what will come next.
writing known words fluently	I write words I know by heart quickly and neatly.
self-monitoring for meaning in writing	I reread my work and listen closely to make sure what I wrote makes sense.

Figure 2.3
Some Common Goals Translated into Focus Phrases

a second opinion! When we seek treatment, we expect our doctors to examine us closely before deciding what needs to be addressed. After all, without really looking into what's causing our pain, how can they even begin to treat it correctly?

Likewise, to plot an effective course of intervention for readers and writers, we have to take a close look at their needs. Diagnostic assessments such as running records, work samples, checklists, screeners, and inventories support our work toward this end. These assessments, given before instruction, allow us an opportunity to examine our student strengths and needs closely so that we can find our focus and clarify where we're going.

My sister-in-law called me one night upset because my nephew was having trouble in his first-grade reading class. Like many parents, she wasn't sure how to help him, so she called in a favor from her support system.

"Can you work with him?" she pleaded. "He can't read."

"What's the problem?" I asked.

Confused, she wondered, "Well . . . what do you mean?"

"I mean . . . what did his teacher say he needed to work on?"

"She didn't say . . . She just said he can't read."

I invited them over the following Saturday morning. I read with him, took several running records, asked him to write for me, and observed the way he worked with sounds. What I found surprised me. He had lots of strengths, but was having difficulties reading on level because he wasn't coordinating those strengths to help himself.

It turned out he was reading under the common first grader's misconception that you have to know every word by heart before you can read them. Often, when he came to a word he didn't know, he just skipped it. In the end, I decided to spend some time with him on applying his strong sense of meaning to solve unknown words while reading. Together, we practiced using pictures to think about what would make sense when he got to words he didn't know. Once he got the hang of that, we worked on using the sounds in the word to double-check his attempts. Before long, with these clarified instructional goals, he was catching up with his first-grade peers.

The understanding that comes from diagnostic assessments allows us to adjust our focus based on the actual needs of our learners. Even when we're faced with ambiguous pleas such as "He can't read" or larger goals mandated by our district, state, or national curriculum, assessing our students to see specifically what they need allows us to customize our focus so we can make informed decisions about exactly where we need to go next.

Assessment and scaffolding go hand in hand. Recall that scaffolding rests in the zone of proximal development, and the only way to know if we're in that zone is to gather enough information through assessment to get a clear picture of the learner's strengths and needs. In their book *Assessment in Perspective*, authors Clare Landrigan and Tammy Mulligan (2013) remind us that "assessment is a window into understanding how our readers are approaching a text and what is confusing to them. It is through observing their actions and noting their responses that we understand how we need to teach them" (12).

Not only can assessment help us home in on our exact focus as mentioned earlier, but it is also key in helping us determine a starting place from which to map our instruction. One of the easiest ways to throw your instructional focus off track is to begin without a clear idea of where your learners are.

TRIANGULATING DATA

The question "Where are we now?" is rooted in assessment, and choosing the right measurement for the job can be a daunting task. Since using only one source of data can be limiting, Landrigan and Mulligan (2013) describe the variety of assessments available to us (see Figure 2.4) and take us back to the idea of triangulating data as a useful way to merge all the information we have on a student to help us make effective planning decisions. When we triangulate data, we gather multiple types of assessment information from various intervals to frame the most accurate picture of our students' needs.

For instance, if I'm setting out to work with Simone to address her teacher's fluency concerns, I can make better planning decisions by looking at a range of data from various moments in time to help me see her reading behaviors more clearly and figure out where to start. I could search through her small-group running records over the past few months, look for fluency indicators on her fall and winter reading inventories, run through her weekly timed reading chart, and check all that against individual conference notes her teacher has been keeping all year. The more data I can add to my picture of Simone as a reader, the clearer my focus becomes.

Since consulting only one piece of assessment paints an incomplete picture, triangulating data will help you make sure that you're building and launching your scaffolds with as much information about the learner as you can gather. With this clarified understanding, you can make effective instructional decisions to move your students forward.

CASE STUDIES

Reviewing a wide range of data on an individual child helps us develop a richer understanding of that child and her needs. Similarly, discussing case studies with a group of friends or peers can open up thoughts and ideas that might not have occurred to us if we had been working on our own. Learning to triangulate data takes time and practice—lots of time and practice. Anytime you're attempting something new and difficult, it makes sense to gather a group of friends to practice with.

ASSESSMENT	WHAT IS IT?	EXAMPLE
Formal	Standardized measures that score achievement and compare broad group performance	• State tests • Achievement tests • Words Their Way
Informal	Give specific information about how learners are performing based on the content in the classroom	• Student work samples • Conference notes • Conversations
Quantitative	Based in numerical measurements that are reliable and can be analyzed and compared statistically	• Psychometric tests • High-stakes tests • State tests
Qualitative	Relates to behaviors and patterns, this type of assessment concerns itself largely with the human as opposed to the number	• Observations • Interviews
Diagnostic	Given before instruction to identify strengths and weaknesses and plan instruction	• Pretests • High-frequency word lists • Reading inventories
Formative	Administered during learning as part of classroom procedures to help the teacher make "in-the-moment" instructional adjustments	• Surveys • Observation • Running records • Student work
Summative	Used primarily after instruction has occurred or at set intervals along the way to measure growth or understanding	• High-stakes tests • Standardized tests • Final exams

*Adapted from Chapter 2 of *Assessment in Perspective* (Landrigan and Mulligan 2013)

Figure 2.4
Using multiple types of assessment can help us find a starting place and fine-tune our focus. Note: Landrigan and Mulligan make a distinct point that various forms of assessment can fall into multiple categories. For instance, running records can be informal, qualitative, quantitative, diagnostic, formative, and summative. Many of the examples I've listed will fall under other assessment categories as well.

As a staff developer, I often lead case studies with teaching teams, but you don't have to wait for your instructional coach to initiate them. They can be done with any group of peers who want to hone their skills around exploring data and making stronger instructional decisions. The process is fairly simple, but the benefits you'll gain will go a long way toward helping you tighten the focus on your instructional goals. And the more often you meet, the better you'll become.

Case studies answer the question "Where are we now?" by looking at multiple pieces of data through multiple lenses. When doctors are in training, they often do similar case studies where a list of symptoms and information are shared about a patient and the group of interns analyze the data, ask further questions, and then share possible diagnoses and treatment plans. Instructional case studies are similar.

Once you've established a group of peers you'll work with, plan to meet with them on a regular basis. Each time you meet, every member of the group brings information about one student to discuss. Teachers frequently bring concerns about students they're finding difficult to accelerate to get a supportive second opinion. It's helpful to gather as much data as you can: running records, writing samples, anecdotal notes, progress monitoring data—anything that can enlighten the group about how your learner is performing.

To get started, go around the group, one member at a time, charting your data on the board in the first two sections of the three-column chart shown in Figure 2.5 (and also available in Figure 2.6). The presenting teacher plots and shares data from as many sources as possible to highlight the student's strong points first (strengths) and then weak areas (concerns). Next, group members discuss the presented data and ask clarifying questions as needed. Then together, they prioritize concerns to identify a list of possible learning goals the presenting teacher might consider as well as some instructional techniques that might be beneficial.

In this case study example of a third grader, the team had several areas of growth to consider. In the end, they decided it might be best to prioritize the instructional focus to support this reader in noticing when his miscues didn't make sense and then to coach him to use his efficient decoding abilities to address the problem when he notices it, leaving the other concerns to deal with later.

STRENGTHS	CONCERNS	PRIORITIZED NEXT STEPS
✓ High effort levels ✓ Instructional text level N, approaching O ✓ Words per minute = 120 WPM ✓ Can break upper-level words when directed ✓ Prefers nonfiction	Resists reading May read too quickly Errors don't always make sense Comprehension is inconsistent Lacks cadence and phrasing when reading	1. Work on monitoring reading to notice when his attempts don't make sense. 2. Bring in word-solving strengths to support self-correcting nonmeaningful errors. 3. Consider slowing down reading for phrasing to support monitoring meaning.

Figure 2.5
Sample Case Study Data Chart

Teachers find this exercise helpful because it gives them an opportunity to see their students' needs through the eyes of their teaching peers, frequently leaving with a better perception of the data and a new understanding of their learner. Exploring their teaching decisions with a community of like-minded thinkers helps them see their instructional goal with clarity and focus.

Figure 2.6 Blank Case Study Data Chart

Case Study

Teacher: _____ Student: _____

Grade: _____ Date: _____

1. Gather a group of problem-solving peers.
2. Plan to meet on a regular basis.
3. Each member brings and presents data for one student.
4. Keep the focus on data (formal and informal).
5. Follow the conversation format: strengths first, followed by concerns, and then possible next steps.

STRENGTHS	CONCERNS	PRIORITIZED NEXT STEPS
FIRST, discuss evidence of concepts, skills, and strategies this student controls as well as approximations that show a movement toward mastery.	NEXT, list areas where the student is having difficulty moving forward. What confusions, misunderstandings, or misguided attempts do you notice that seem to be holding things back?	NOW, as a group, discuss the data, ask follow-up questions, and think about instructional moves that would help this student. Prioritize these next steps into a plan of action.

The effectiveness of our scaffolds can be directly tied to the clarity of our focus. Remember, there is power in specificity. Indistinct learning goals only stall our planning, frustrate us, derail our instruction—and, worst of all, confuse our students. Simply put, if we aren't clear, our learners aren't clear. Too often, we misinterpret a student's uncertainty as inability or resistance, when the problem actually lies in a lack of clarity on our part.

Getting focused, then, is the first domino. It sets the tone for our scaffolds and lays the groundwork for how well they will fall into place. To constructively guide learners across the zone of proximal development, we must be clear about exactly where we are and where we're going.

Only then can we begin to plot a direct course to get there.

CONSTRUCTIVE REFLECTIONS

1. Recall one of your lessons that didn't go the way you'd hoped. How directly did the clarity of your focus relate to the success of your lesson?

2. Can you think of a time when a related goal (as opposed to being directly relevant) skewed the effectiveness of your instruction?

3. When you're faced with a reader who's hard to advance, what assessment data do you find most useful in pinpointing your focus?

4. Reflect on one of your most recent lessons. Would an outside observer have been able to identify your focus? What if he were blindfolded? What if he were wearing earplugs?

5. Think about a learning objective you find difficult to zero in on. If a miracle happened while you were away and you returned to find your students had mastered it, what's the first thing you would notice? What would you see? What would you hear?

6. What would it be like for you to gather a few peers and form a case study group? Who would you invite? Which students' data would you bring to discuss?

CHAPTER 3 STAYING FOCUSED:
DESIGNING A PLAN AND KEEPING THE GOAL IN SIGHT

"Road trip!"

Back in college, these two words were all it took to kick off a crazy (often misguided) weekend of fun with friends.

It usually started off, as these things do, with several of us chatting about a particular place or an upcoming event, and before long, someone in the group would yell, "Road trip!" and it'd be on. No questions asked. Back then, when someone yelled "Road trip," you just went. We always knew our destination, our goal, but it was rare that we'd actually stop to think about how we were going to get there. We weren't about details. More often than not, we'd all just pile into someone's mother's car and hit the road—careless and free, trusting we'd figure out the details along the way.

Those were the days, right?

That doesn't happen now. I'm all grown up. Don't get me wrong; I still love a road trip. Ask any of my friends. But my approach is different. Back then we were less concerned with where we'd stay, what we'd eat, or even how we'd get there. We weren't very intentional about much at all. Now my time is limited. I have grown-up things to tend to—bills to pay, people counting on me, and a job to get back to. As an adult, I'm more thoughtful about such things. I need a plan.

When I think about my teaching career, I matured in much the same way. When I started out, I taught everything as if someone had yelled "Road trip!"— and off I'd go. I remember the first time I taught inferring word meanings. It was my first year, and my team leader announced that the entire third grade would be teaching context clues for the next few weeks. *Road trip!* I had no clue what I was doing. I knew what context clues were, I had some inkling of what they could look like instructionally, and I was excited to say the least. But beyond that? Nothing.

We got off to an acceptable start (luckily, they'd done it in second grade), but before long we'd made so many pit stops for refills, stalls, and random distractions that I spent most of the time just trying to get us back on track. I was oblivious. I knew where we were going, but I had no clue how we were going to get there.

This struggle isn't at all uncommon. I learned the hard way that although a goal gives us a destination, it doesn't map out how we'll get there. These days, I can enjoy a road trip more now that I've learned the basics of traveling and planning, and effective instructional scaffolds depend on this same approach. After your internal GPS has determined where you're going and aligns this with where you are now, it moves to ask the next important question:

- What's the best way to get there?

Once we've fine-tuned our focus with an accurate understanding of the goal, we can begin to plot our course. A few years ago, I worked with several teachers on my campus to explore ways we could become more clearly focused about the needs of our learners. As part of this staff development they'd spent several hours looking at student data both individually with me and in case study teams. By the time we were finished, I was pleased to see that several of them were able to identify specific focal points for their neediest readers. I was even more pleased when, that same afternoon, three of those teachers stopped by my room separately, all with a similar concern: "Okay, now I know this. I can see it clearly. But . . . how do I make it happen?"

It's a pivotal experience in the scaffolding process when we arrive at the stage where we finally ask the million-dollar question: "How do I craft specific instruction to teach that?" Beyond knowing what kids need to learn. Beyond figuring out where they are in the continuum. "How do I make that happen?"

Well, you'll need a plan.

GETTING THERE: GRADUAL RELEASE THROUGH THE 5S PROGRESSION

Preparing ahead gives us a sense of direction and is a crucial technique in our drive to stay focused. Recall our discussion of the gradual release of responsibility model in Chapter 1. Because of the way this familiar model's *I do/We do/You do* progression supports us in maintaining a deliberate focus throughout the teaching process (see Figure 3.1), it claims a spot as one of the leading ways we scaffold learners. Its sequence from *modeled instruction* to *guided practice* to *independent practice* gives us a basic map as we proactively cut a direct path through the zone of proximal development from point A to point B. This map provides a backbone for our scaffolding efforts. It gives us the structure.

TEACHER RESPONSIBILITY		STUDENT RESPONSIBILITY
Modeling (I do)	Guided Practice (We do)	Independent Practice (You do)

Figure 3.1
The Gradual Release of Responsibility Model

Given that our intention here is to focus on scaffolding from the perspective of the more knowing other, I've magnified the individual components of the gradual release model so we can look at them through that particular lens. This extended view, called the 5S progression (Figure 3.2), builds on the structure of the classic model to emphasize five actionable steps that highlight the specific role we play in moving learners to independence. To that end, its verbs—*show, share, support, sustain*, and *survey*—signify the actions of the more knowing other throughout the gradual release progression. Certainly, students are active in this process as well and eventually become solely responsible for the learning goal, but an awareness of our role as we work with young readers and writers will remind us to stay intentional about our teaching and focused on our instructional bull's-eye.

- *Show*—(modeled instruction/I do)—The teacher models and clearly explains the new learning.

- *Share*—(guided practice/we do)—Though still largely in control, the teacher begins to hand over the new learning, essentially sharing the responsibility with the learner.

- *Support*—(guided practice/we do)—Continuing to share the load, the teacher pulls back while supporting the learner in taking on greater degrees of the responsibility for the learning and offering support as needed.

- *Sustain*—(independent practice/you do)—The teacher creates opportunities and sustains an environment that nurtures the learner's efforts to independently take on the full load of the learning.

- *Survey*—(assessment)—Throughout the process—before, during, and after—the teacher is in a state of continual assessment, watching and observing, to ensure that the work is solidly within the learner's zone of proximal development, instruction is on course, and, at every step along the way, the student is being given the most responsibility for the learning possible.

TEACHER RESPONSIBILITY			STUDENT RESPONSIBILITY
Modeling (I do)	Guided Practice (We do)		Independent Practice (You do)
Show	Share	Support	Sustain
		Survey	

Figure 3.2
The 5S Progression

For instance, say Ms. Davis wants to teach her class to create mental images to support their comprehension. She could model (*show*) a particular visualization strategy across several read-alouds, and then invite the class to mirror her actions (*share*) as they try it with a common piece of text. She could then withdraw a little and offer assistance as they practice visualizing while reading alone or in collaborative groups (*support*), and then finally pull back completely as she continues to orchestrate opportunities for students to take over creating mental images (*sustain*) on their own without her support. At every stage—not just the end—Ms. Davis would be checking their progress (*survey*) to make sure students are ready for the next stage and, eventually, for independence.

Perhaps the most significant difference between the gradual release model and 5S progression is the role of assessment (survey). Because it isn't clearly singled out as part of the traditional GRRM sequence—and largely because of misunderstandings and misinterpretations of the model itself—assessment often takes a backseat to the more recognized aspects of the model. As a result, and despite its inherent function as a fundamental element in the gradual release process, many discussions of ongoing assessment within the gradual release model are lacking. In light of this, the survey component of the 5S progression highlights this important aspect. Because it's about being observant and, more specifically, being a kid watcher, *survey* encompasses all forms of assessment (see Figure 2.4 on page 31). We'll return to this critical practice of surveying shortly with a deeper look at how doing so can give us in-the-moment information to help keep our scaffolds on track.

The five actions within the 5S progression also serve as a planning map of sorts as they steer us to think intentionally about exactly what we'll do at each stage of the gradual release process. If you're looking for direction in planning your scaffolds, you might find it helpful to ask yourself the following guiding questions as you prepare your lessons:

- *What specifically will I* show *my learner? How exactly will I explain it?*

- *How will I begin to* share *the responsibility with my learner? What will that look like?*

- *In what ways will I* support *my learner in a move toward greater independence?*

- *How will I* sustain *an environment that allows and encourages my learner to practice independently?*

- *How and when will I* survey *the effectiveness of my instruction along the way? How will I know where to start? How will I know when to move to the next level? How will I measure success when we're finished?*

For instance, recall our second-grade readers from Chapter 2 who were learning to run the bases across words. After I identified the instructional goal (*survey*), I decided to model what I meant as soon as I finished introducing the focus phrase by saying, "Now, watch me run the bases across this word as I read it." I showed them what I wanted them to do by covering the word with my finger and then sliding it from left to right, pausing along the way to make sure each of the sounds in the beginning, middle, and end matched what I was saying (*show*). I did this several times, checking as I did so to make sure they understood my modeling (*survey*). Fairly quickly, I invited them in to read words with me—my finger pointing to the top of the word's sounds and sliding from left to right with theirs on the bottom doing the same (*share*). As soon as I could see they had the hang of it (*survey*), I pulled my hand out, leaving them to run the bases on their own, but stood by, ready to reteach if needed (*support*). We lingered with this practice until they seemed to be getting it (*survey*), and then I prompted them to run the bases with just their eyes, removing their finger from the text, again with me standing by in case they got into trouble (*support*). Over the next several lessons, I watched for specific opportunities where they'd hit a snag and needed me to remind them to run the bases (*survey/support*). Eventually, the readers required my reminders less and less frequently, so I dropped my cues completely, continuing to meet with them several more times to give them opportunities to strengthen their new skill (*sustain*). A final running record verified my confidence that the readers were independently matching the sounds across words as they read (*survey*).

In Figure 3.3, notice the intentional decision making involved in relation to this lesson progression and the planning questions discussed earlier. You'll find a similar planning chart in Figure 3.4 to use as you think through the actions you'll take in your own instructional scaffolds. I'm not suggesting you write this out for each and every lesson you plan. However, I do suggest you try it when you're faced with a difficult concept or struggling to move some learners who are having a harder time advancing. Writing through this process as you plan, even periodically, will solidify these questions and the thinking they require in your mental stores. As they become part of the internal dialogue you have with yourself, you'll notice your planning becoming more effective and your instruction staying directly relevant to your learning goal with increasing frequency.

We'll revisit this model and more tools to support it as we continue to explore the construction zone. But for now, with its sequence serving as an enhanced reflection of the gradual release progression through the lens of the more knowing other, the 5S progression can help us make the connection between *where we are now* and *where we're going* as we intentionally map out the *best way to get there* (see Figure 3.5).

THE 5S PROGRESSION WITH LAUREN'S SECOND-GRADE READERS	
<u>Show</u> What specifically will I show to my learner? How will I explain it?	Model sliding finger across word from left to right and making the sounds match while checking for meaning.
<u>Share</u> How will I begin to share the responsibility with my learner? What will that look like?	Invite students to run the bases with teacher finger guiding on top and student finger following along on bottom.
<u>Support</u> In what ways will I support my learner in a move toward greater independence?	Guide students as they run the bases with finger independently and eventually run the bases without using their finger.
<u>Sustain</u> How will I sustain an environment for my learner to practice independently?	Monitor students for independence in small-group lessons and individual reading workshop conferences.
<u>Survey</u> How and when will I survey the effectiveness of my instruction along the way? How will I know where to start? How will I measure success when we're finished?	Administer regular running records, observe, and keep ongoing teacher lesson notes on readers' word-solving strategies.

Figure 3.3
5S Planning Chart

Figure 3.4   Blank 5S Planning Chart

Planning with the 5S Progression

Teacher: _____

Instructional Goal: _____

Student(s): _____

ACTION STEP	THINK ABOUT…	NOTES
SHOW	What specifically will I show my learner(s)? How will I explain it?	
SHARE	How will I begin to share the responsibility with my learner(s)? What would that look like?	
SUPPORT	In what ways will I support my learner(s) in moving toward greater independence?	
SUSTAIN	How will I sustain an environment for my learner(s) to continue to practice independently?	
SURVEY	How and when will I survey the effectiveness of my instruction along the way? How will I know where to start and when to move to the next level? And how will I measure success when we're finished?	

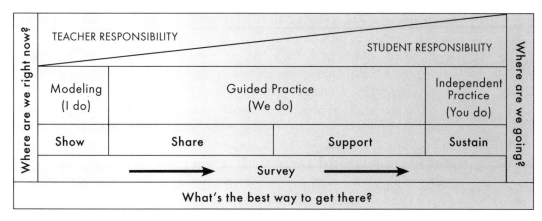

Figure 3.5
The 5S Progression—The Hub of the Instructional GPS

SURVEY: USING ONGOING ASSESSMENT TO STAY FOCUSED

How many times have you started a lesson reasonably well, only to finish with your instruction entirely off course? This happens to all of us, because clarifying and planning for a learning goal is only the beginning. Effective scaffolders regularly monitor their teaching to make sure their instructional moves remain clearly connected to their intended focus. To maintain that focus, we teach in a constant state of assessment—surveying the effects of our instruction, making sure we're still on track, and avoiding diversions along the way that might derail us.

With the fifth tenet of the 5S progression, *survey*, we're reminded that ongoing evaluation before, during, and afterward is vital to ensure that our scaffolds stay on track. Although this certainly includes the more formal ways in which we assess students, it also incorporates informal assessments and observations along the way. Waiting until after you've taught a concept to see how well your students grasped it may be common practice for some, but if that's the only time you check the oil, you might be disappointed at what you find.

One way to make sure you're continually monitoring the progress of your scaffolds is to intentionally mark out several points in time where you'll survey how things are progressing. Knowing ahead of time how and when you'll check in will keep you mindful and help you stay focused. For instance, I work with many teachers who make it their regular practice to do a quick running record on one student as they begin their small-group reading instruction (rotating to different readers with each lesson). You could just as easily schedule checkpoints at particular moments in your time line as you shift stages in the scaffolding progression or as an ongoing part of your regular routine.

Another practical way to continually survey the effectiveness of your scaffolds is to get in the habit of taking notes during your instruction. For many of you, this is a lot harder than it sounds. Taking notes while trying to teach may feel unnatural and even difficult as you begin, and it can certainly get messy at first, but in time you'll develop a system and a routine that works for you. As a ritual part of your teaching practices, the physical act of observing and jotting down things you notice throughout your lesson can help you stay focused on your learners and their response to your instruction.

If you still find this challenging, you aren't alone. Often one of the reasons we struggle to take notes is that we freeze under the assumption that they have to be perfect. In this case, it may help to know that your notes don't have to be perfect, nor do they have to be teeming with earth-shattering revelations. Your notes are for you. They inform your instruction, and as long as you find them valuable, they're fine.

Teachers also struggle to keep records because they're concentrating so hard on the interactive aspects of instruction that they can't always manage the physical act of note taking at the same time. This is especially true with new teachers or anyone who isn't in the habit of taking notes on the run. In this case, you might try planning to jot some quick thoughts during the few moments immediately after the lesson. Over time, in anticipation of these moments, you'll likely find yourself unconsciously jotting notes as you teach—and before long, taking notes on the run will become a ritual part of your instruction.

A more fundamental reason teachers resist taking notes is that they aren't quite sure what exactly to take notes on. To help manage your written records a little better and make them more useful for you at the same time, consider limiting your notes to the specific focus and plan for the lesson you're teaching—and let everything else go. Tie your notes directly to what you are trying to accomplish. Ask yourself these questions:

- What am I noticing with specific relevance to the final goal?

- What do I want to remember as a celebration of movement toward that goal?

- What do I want to remember as an area to work on?

- What surprised me and will need to be tended to before we can move forward?

A character in George Bernard Shaw's *Man and Superman* praises the sensibility of his tailor for measuring him each and every time he sees him. Just like a tailor's frequent measuring, assessment in the scaffolding process is critical and recursive. In addition to checking in and taking notes, effective teachers cultivate the scaffolding process through a constant mind-set of assessment. In this way, we internalize assessment as a frame of mind—an organic, fluid activity that's an inseparable part of our interaction with our students. Each time we work, we measure again to see where we are.

As we move learners through the zone of proximal development, surveying the process through ongoing assessment and reflection allows us to check in at the various stages of scaffolding to see if we need to stay longer, retrace our steps, or move forward. Particularly sensitive to the ways students respond to our instruction, we anticipate the next, most effective instructional moves that will keep our efforts on track. We're constantly on the lookout. Constantly evaluating. Constantly surveying. Our scaffolds depend on it.

AVOIDING DISTRACTIONS THAT THROW OUR SCAFFOLDS OFF COURSE

Have you ever found yourself just seconds away from an outright assault on your car's GPS system because you made a wrong turn somehow and its annoying robot voice keeps repeating, "Recalculating . . . Please make a legal U-turn . . . Recalculating . . . Please make a legal U-turn"? Though frustrating in the moment, it can be comforting to know that someone (or rather, some machine) is minding the map to make sure we arrive at our destination. This is one of the most useful design elements of a GPS system: after it has asked those original guiding questions to figure out *where we're headed* in comparison with *where we are right now* and then maps the *best course* for us, it continues to ask along the way, *What do we do if we get off track?*

Let's face it: sometimes teaching gets difficult, we lose our way, and we struggle to keep up. When we make a wrong turn while scaffolding, we count on our instructional GPS to kick in and help us recalculate our sense of direction. To this end, we continually survey whether what we're doing is still relevant to the learning goal we identified in the beginning. If not, we quickly get ourselves back on track so we can head, once again, straight for the bull's-eye. Here, we turn our attention toward looking out for diversions and distractions that keep us from staying focused.

UNCERTAIN TIME LINES

I find it incredibly interesting that instructional goals are rarely accompanied by any sort of time line. Think about it. Our state and national curricula are fairly clear about *what* to teach, but, besides the customary end-of-the-year deadline, they don't give us much direction on *when* to teach it. This can be problematic.

For instance, in an effort to meet the standard of "reading increasingly more difficult texts," our first-grade readers are expected to be able to read a text level J by the time they leave in May. In August, that end-of-the-year J seems so far away, it's barely a blip on our radar. But it's coming. And it's coming fast. If we aren't prepared for it, it can sneak up on us, and when it does, it'll derail us without fail.

Staying aware of our time line helps us stay focused. Proactively we ask ourselves, "If my kids need to be reading a J by May, what do they need to be reading by October? What about December and February?" My colleagues and I find it helpful to mark out a time line with micro goals along the way to keep us on target as we move toward our final goal.

Without a clear time line, it's easy to linger too long, meander, and get off track. To adjust for this, ask yourself these questions during the planning stages:

- How much time will I need to meet this goal?

- How much time do I anticipate this taking?

- How will I monitor to make sure we're still on schedule?

LOSING SIGHT OF THE GOAL

Another reason we lose focus is a result of limits in our instructional vision. This occurs most often during the planning stages but can also creep up during our delivery, and happens in three ways that are similar to troubles we sometimes experience with our physical vision:

- *Nearsightedness*: We're so focused on the immediate steps, we lose sight of the larger vision.

- *Farsightedness*: We're fully aware of the larger goal but struggle to coordinate the smaller steps to get us there.

- *Double Vision*: Our vision gets blurred, we can see multiple paths, and in our indecisiveness, we never pick a clear direction.

A few summers ago, I worked with some second-grade teachers as they sat down to plan their first week's word study block. Their curriculum dictated the following goal: identify the difference between a vowel and a consonant. Relieved to start off with such a seemingly straightforward concept and pointing out that the kids had covered the goal in first grade, the team quickly planned to teach a fun song that would help their students distinguish vowels from consonants.

"That sounds like a great place to start, but hold on a second," I cautioned. "What exactly *is* the difference between a vowel and a consonant?"

"Well, *a, e, i, o,* and *u* are the vowels (and sometimes *y*)—and all the rest are consonants!" they chimed in matter-of-factly.

"Yes," I pushed. "But how are they *different*?"

This example of nearsightedness almost threw our focus. Had we been content teaching the song, our readers would have definitely been able to *identify* their vowels (and conversely, their consonants), but beyond that, they wouldn't have been able to tell us how they're *different*. And those differences, like how a vowel opens the mouth and a consonant closes it, are important foundations to the higher-level word study goals their students would be attacking later in the year, such as open versus closed syllabication, vowel patterns in spelling, and long versus short vowels in decoding to support the meaning of texts.

When we can't see clearly, it's incredibly easy to lose our way. A deep investigation of our instructional goal can certainly take some effort, but strong scaffolds require our looking at them from all angles so we can craft instruction that best supports our learners.

TRYING TO TEACH TOO MUCH AT ONCE

The well-known theorem citing a straight line as the shortest distance between two points may serve the purpose in geometry, but finding that straight line in scaffolding can present quite a puzzle. That's because the path across the zone of proximal development isn't a concrete, flat surface. Scaffolding is an intricate process, and zeroing in on the exact direction you'll go can get confusing. More often than not, your learning goal will intertwine with other important learning concepts that run in front of, behind, and simultaneously alongside of it. Sorting it all out can get difficult, and doing so unsuccessfully is another classic way to skew your focus.

Unaware, it's not unusual for us to bite off more than we can chew when what we really need to do is narrow our target a bit further. As my friend Helen likes to remind me, "We're building a scaffold, not a cable bridge." When we break our goals down into manageable chunks, we can see them clearly and teach toward them more effectively.

Consider the common learning goal of summarizing fiction. At first glance, this seems like a fairly clear-cut objective. But when you investigate it more closely, you'll notice a time line of other concepts that you'll need to tend to. It might be easier to think of them as mini-scaffolds within a larger one. Think about all the scaffolding that will be required for learners to be able to summarize fiction. We'll need to make sure they can identify elements of fiction, such as characters and plot, and that they can identify them in texts that they've read. Additionally, they'll need to be taught to bring all those elements together to retell stories chronologically. Once they can retell stories successfully, they'll need to learn to summarize by condensing those retellings while thinking about theme and author's purpose.

This is no small feat. All of these smaller scaffolds (and likely more I haven't mentioned) will need to be addressed. The shortest distance between the beginning and end points in a scaffold may not always be the quickest or the easiest ways to get where we need to go. Learning standards usually require an integrated series of subscaffolds to reach them. When we prioritize these smaller steps toward the larger objective, and tend to other, time-sensitive goals that need to be reached before it, we keep things manageable and our focus stays clear.

GETTING OVERWHELMED BY NEEDS

Another time we might take on more than we can manage is when we're working with learners whose needs overwhelm us and we aren't sure what to address first. This can be especially true with our hard-to-advance readers and writers—everything seems so important.

A few years ago, Josh called me in to observe one of his first-grade small groups. He asked for specific feedback on ways he could make his instruction as effective as possible in the small amount of time he had with them. With a strong focus and a clear plan, his lesson started off without a hitch. Josh was working with his lowest readers on one-to-one voice matching to print, so I looked for clear evidence of instruction toward that goal. What I noticed was a lot of strong teaching. But the lesson seemed scattered, and Josh spent very little time working with his readers on one-to-one matching.

After the lesson, we looked over my observation notes together. In my notes, I'd blocked off a section and written his focus over it: "One-to-One Matching." I asked Josh what he noticed.

"Well, it looks like I did some good stuff and I stayed on target time wise [he'd been working on that], and I was able to read with every one of the kids in the group and everybody stayed on task [he'd been working on those as well]. But . . . what's this? Oh. It looks like I didn't really teach much on the one-to-one matching."

"Yeah," I said. "I noticed that, too. Talk about how that happened."

Josh went on to share his concerns for this group and how every time he worked with them, he couldn't get through his lesson because they seemed so needy. He felt like he was constantly shifting gears to address their needs during their groups and was left feeling like he hadn't really accomplished much at all.

"I want to fix everything!" he said.

No doubt you've felt this same way. We all have. To help, I suggested that Josh keep a "For Later" list next to his small-group planning binder. If he encountered an instructional need that felt important while working with his group, he could relieve some mental pressure by writing it on his list. Other than that, he would stick with his original plan. Then later, when he sat down to write out the next series of lessons, he could use his For Later list to prioritize his next steps. Within a few days, Josh dropped in to say that things were looking up: he was able to stay focused without fear that he'd forget to cover something big.

For Later lists work well for small-group instruction, whole-group lessons, and even individual conferences. If something feels pressing but isn't in line with your instructional focus, consider saving it for later. Yes, some confusions do need to be addressed immediately, but most can wait. Trying to fix everything at once will only end up distracting you from your goal. Stick with your plan and come back to it later.

MISTAKING BIRD WALKING FOR A TEACHABLE MOMENT

During one of my first official evaluations, I was devastated to find that I'd been marked down because one of my students brought up some vaguely connected notion that took our lesson in a completely different direction. In the post-observation conference, I learned there was a name for this.

"You let that student bird-walk your lesson," my principal said, referring to the incident. "You can't let that happen."

"Bird walking?" I countered, fairly certain that bird walking wasn't a real thing. "That wasn't bird walking. That was a teachable moment!" I went on to give an amazing, almost Oscar-worthy speech about how it was my job to inspire curiosity in my students and honor their search for answers. I'm not sure, but I think I even punctuated it all by standing up and pointing my finger to the sky.

Probably just to put an end to my rant, she conceded and adjusted my rating. But over time, I've come to realize that she was right about two things: One, bird walking is a real thing. And two, that "teachable moment" I defended as a young teacher so long ago was, in fact, bird walking.

Nonetheless, for years before I accepted that, I hid tons of misguided and off-focus lessons behind the sanctimonious curtain of a "teachable moment." But there really is a difference. And knowing this difference can help you make sure your instructional plan isn't unintentionally hijacked.

Bird walking, it turns out, is when we allow random comments, questions, and thoughts to derail our focus. This can be difficult, because we really do want to cultivate curiosity in our learners and we do want to make room for their pursuit of it. And if scaffolding really is about co-construction of knowledge like we've been saying all along, doesn't it make sense that we'd follow their needs?

Yes, but the difference lies, as always, in our intention behind it. We have to stay mindful. Simply put, a true teachable moment will follow the learner and *at the same time* support and enhance your scaffold's instructional focus.

Bird walking will do everything it can to take you away from it.

REMOVING SCAFFOLDS TOO SOON

Sometimes, despite our best intentions, we don't so much lose our focus as discontinue it too soon. I realize this could get confusing, because the fundamental intent behind scaffolds is to deconstruct them once the learning goal has been met. It's true. We don't want to linger with a scaffold for longer than necessary, but neither do we want to bring it to a screeching halt before the job is done.

Lots of times, as we begin to see our students being successful, we start to pull back (which we should do to release responsibility) and then, fueled by a rising sense of triumph, we hastily relax our focus—and the scaffold falls apart. Ironically, this is when we need to keep our focus the tightest. We're almost there!

Be careful not to drop the ball as you get closer to the goal. When we find ourselves having to retrace our steps to figure out where the breakdown occurred on our way to a learning goal we thought was already mastered, our confusion makes it difficult to regain our focus and correct the issue. We end up missing the bull's-eye completely.

INVITATION ONLY

Josh's earlier invitation for me to give him feedback on his instruction brings up a powerful way you can watch for distractors and keep your focus in check. Two heads are truly better than one, and when we invite another set of eyes in to help us monitor our work, our vision gets that much clearer.

If you have one, every literacy coach I know would jump at the chance to support you in this way and would do so constructively. But if a coach isn't available or you're simply not quite ready for that, what about a trusted friend? I once worked on a campus that held what they called walkabouts—a tradition where teachers could walk around the building observing one another in an intentional way. Even if your campus doesn't schedule regular walkabouts, I imagine you could still swing a peer observation. Most administrators would support you without hesitation once you've explained the process and your purpose behind it.

Admittedly, inviting someone in to watch you teach might be disconcerting for some of you, but try to keep an open mind. A lot of teachers resist this model for fear the observer will draw attention to flaws in their work. But just as Josh named specifically what he needed feedback on, giving your observer a clear objective might help alleviate that concern. For instance, to guide someone in helping you stay focused, you might use the following questions:

- Can you clearly determine my focus by observing my instructional moves?

- Does every step of my instruction stay relevant to my goal?

- Do you notice anything that keeps me from my objective?

When set up in a structured and supportive professional environment, peer observations can be an effective way to help you clarify and keep your focus.

When we know for certain what we're teaching toward, exactly what our students need from us, and precisely where we'll take them, we've taken the first steps toward building empowering scaffolds.

Staying focused during our planning and teaching not only keeps our attention on the instructional side of the scaffold, but also keeps our students engaged on the learning side of the scaffold. The more concise we are, the better students can follow our direction toward the learning goal. The less precise we are, the more confused they will be.

But even with the best of intentions—a good plan in place and a deliberate mind-set to stay on course—we will encounter unexpected bumps along the way. Things will break down. Problems will occur. And sometimes, the course we've so carefully plotted will need some adjustments.

In the next chapter, we'll discuss bringing some flexibility into our focus so that we can recognize when this happens and when we need to change course.

CONSTRUCTIVE REFLECTIONS

1. Can you think of a time when a lesson derailed as a direct result of imprecise planning on your part? How did you feel? How did your students respond? What could you have done differently?

2. How do you monitor whether you're wandering off point instructionally? What routines might you establish to help you keep an eye on this?

3. This chapter introduced the concept of the 5S progression as an enhanced expression of the traditional gradual release of responsibility model. How are the two formats alike? What are their major differences? How do the two exist in conjunction with each other?

4. The *survey* element of the 5S progression suggests that you teach in a constant mind-set of assessment. What does that mean to you personally? What instructional shifts might you make to be more intentional about ongoing assessment?

5. This chapter ends with a discussion of several distractions that keep us from staying focused. Which of these resonate with you the most? Which snags will prompt you to deeper self-reflection around them?

6. What would it be like for you to invite an observer in to give you feedback on your focus? Do you already have a supportive friend or instructional coach who could do this for you? If so, what keeps you from inviting them in? If not, who could you identify as a supportive peer to offer a consulting point of view?

PART TWO

FLEXIBILITY

Tethered to our focus, our scaffolds have a responsive, organic quality and shift with perfect timing to meet the specific needs of our learners.

CHAPTER 4 FLEXIBLE DESIGN:
PLANNING INSTRUCTION WITH AN OPEN MIND

Effective instruction is different for different people in different situations. What works for one of us may not work for the teacher next door and may not even work with next year's students. On the other hand, that same instructional move might work for half our class but not the other. It really all depends on who's doing the teaching, who's doing the learning, and how they work together.

This is something you already know.

Still, consider this: at its heart, scaffolding is an interpersonal, human endeavor—and humans are complicated creatures. Recall how scaffolding originally grew out of a social constructivist theory, one that pivots on social interactions between two or more people as they work together to create meaning around a particular concept. Although this may sound simple, it can get incredibly muddled. All of us, teachers and students alike, carry with us the highs and lows of our teaching and learning histories, our assumptions, and our baggage. We're driven by our desires, our motivations, our needs, our wants, our cultures, our hopes, our fears. None of these are concrete, bringing any attempts to squeeze scaffolding into a one-size-fits-all box next to impossible.

What's more, scaffolding involves a relationship between the teacher and student based on all of these things, but raises the stakes by tossing in an instructional goal that may or may not be a priority for either participant.

Throw in a strict time line and a variety of outside opinions about how you're supposed to go about reaching that goal and . . . well, you can see the problem.

In response to this, instructional scaffolding is organic. It grows and moves based on personalities, newly identified needs, in-the-moment information, and each successive interaction between teacher and student. It adjusts for good days and bad days. It follows the teachable moment while maintaining an instructional goal.

It's large and small, simple and complicated, beautiful and messy—all at the same time.

This, then, sets the stage for the second common condition of scaffolding:

Effective scaffolds require flexibility based in the specific needs of the learner.

Our best teaching occurs when we work from a flexible structure with an intentional purpose: we know where we're going and we have a plan, but we allow for necessary detours while simultaneously holding the goal in sight. We can take side journeys and still mind the map. We can linger in certain spots to enjoy the view without getting off track. We can even extend the journey or cut it short, if we decide to, and still have a terrific time.

We can do both.

Instructional scaffolding is grounded in this trade-off. Once we've established our focus, we can orchestrate lessons that maintain the organic and flexible qualities real teaching requires. Acting mindfully from that plan, we can make improvised, decisive moves in a variety of directions that serve our students' learning best—all while keeping our efforts clearly connected to our intended goal.

In this chapter, we'll explore the flexibility of instructional scaffolds as it applies to *designing* instruction and in the following chapter, we'll take a closer look at flexibility in *delivering* it.

FLEXIBLE PLANNING: FINDING THE RIGHT FIT

Remember my unfortunate road-trip attempt to teach third graders to infer using context clues? I was unfocused, unprepared, and struggled to keep the learning on track.

After fumbling my way through that lesson (and too many more like it), anxiety and perfectionism eventually gave way to a structured teaching philosophy that left no room for pit stops or teachable moments. There would be no meandering, no exploring, and no uncertainty. I had my agenda and we were all sticking to it—like it or not!

My teaching became structured to a fault.

That didn't really work either. In no time flat, the ups and downs found in just about every teaching day collided, bringing my well-laid plans to a screeching halt. I quickly learned that a rigid plan with extreme limitations can be something of a buzz kill.

It seemed a compromise was in order.

Students, classes, and needs vary from year to year. No learner or group will require the same level of support, nor will every learning target need to be scaffolded to the nth degree. There are different routes to the same goal, and to support our students effectively, we'll have to stretch our presumptions and be receptive to new possibilities.

One of the first places we learn to be flexible in the construction zone is before we ever start—in the preparation and planning stages. This sets the scene for the entire process. As we plan, we'll want to consider our options carefully. We'll certainly want to think about teaching moves that have proven successful for us in the past, but we'll also need to keep an open mind for a variety of instructional techniques and different ideas that could do the job better.

Writing teacher and consultant Jeff Anderson is fond of saying, "It's a scaffold, not a straitjacket." The key, then, is to allow for flexibility—flexibility in ourselves, in our thinking, and in our scaffolds. As you continue reading, consider the different ways you design lessons and how flexible you are in the way you scaffold instruction.

THINKING FLEXIBLY ABOUT ABSOLUTES

When we demand rigidity, we actually limit what scaffolding can do for our learners. Very few things in life are exactly black or white. Instead, most fall into that gray area somewhere in between—and this is certainly true for teaching. The quickest way to undermine your instructional scaffolds is to work from a mind-set of all-or-nothing thinking like this:

- "I *always* teach it this way . . ."

- "The *only* way to get this across is if I . . ."

- "My kids will *never* . . ."

In these examples, notice how the absolute thoughts leave no room for other options.

As you plan instruction, examine your thinking for words such as *always*, *only*, and *never*. These might be red flags that you're seeing with tunnel vision that limits your scaffolds. Instead, ask yourself these questions:

- Are there other (or different) ways to do this?

- What options might be more effective?

- Who could I consult for more ideas?

What's interesting about absolute thinking is how, most of the time, we aren't even aware that we're doing it. For years, I taught my youngest readers to attend to initial visual cuing by saying, "Look at the first *letter* and think about what would make sense." It never dawned on me that there might be a more effective way to teach this. I wasn't being stubborn. I just thought that was the best way to get my point across. That is, until I observed the teacher next door.

When I watched her work with her readers on the same skill, she phrased it a little differently: "Make the first *sound* and think about what would make sense." It may seem small, but that slight shift in wording makes a big difference. Think about it. Although using the first letter is an efficient skill when it comes to decoding words such as *cat*, *park*, and *take*, it's counterintuitive when readers come across words such as *ship*, *these*, and *chair*. Here, they need to be thinking sounds, not letters. Sure, it may not make a drastic difference in our lowest text levels where the first letter is often enough, but eventually I wanted my readers to decode words in larger sound chunks. For instance, a student who sets out to read the word *ship* one letter at a time is at a huge disadvantage compared with a reader who's been conditioned to look for beginning sounds and, more efficiently, notices the sound of the /sh/ digraph first. This subtle difference between prompting for the first *letter* and prompting for the first *sound* changed my instruction just slightly, but had lasting implications. And, I might never have noticed it if I'd been so bound to my own way of doing things that I hadn't been able to see other possibilities.

Another form of absolute planning that can ruin our scaffolds is polar thinking. Have you ever noticed how some people align so closely with their philosophies and ways of teaching that it's almost like brawling political parties during an election year? Filing into their camps, they shun any ideal but their own:

- phonics versus meaning!

- words per minute versus cadence and phrasing!

- immersion in easy texts versus close reading of challenging texts!

Be cautious with programs or leaders who tell you things such as, "You have to teach it exactly this way" or "This is the only way." Polarities are essentially *either/or* approaches, and they can blind us to other, possibly more effective options. When you're planning your scaffolds, you'll find more success if you keep the open mind of a *both/and* outlook. For instance, we can teach fluency as speed *and* cadence, insist students use phonics *and* meaning to decode, and grow readers through experiences with easy *and* challenging texts. Flexibility in scaffolding dictates that we consider and make room for other positions that may differ from our own. Don't our students deserve as much?

In a career where so much keeps us hopping, we often gravitate toward absolutes because—whether conscious or outside of our awareness—they're comforting. Since they rarely challenge our preconceived notions, absolutes make decisions about our instruction seem easier, somehow making us feel like we're doing a good job. But as Regie Routman reminds us, "It's not about how good I am. It's about how I can meet your needs" (Routman 2011). Despite any false sense of control absolutes might afford, all-or-nothing thinking is the exact opposite of flexibility, stifling our scaffolds and keeping us from seeing new ways to help our learners.

THINKING FLEXIBLY ABOUT RESOURCES

As we design instruction, two major components we'll need to figure out are the activities we'll do and the resources that will support them, and being inflexible about either of those can stall our work. We all have certain materials we return to year after year, but when we're partial to a tried-and-true favorite that's worked for us before, we can become incredibly rigid about it.

A sure sign of resource rigidity is selecting materials and activities before fleshing out the learning goal and how your learners connect to it. When I plan with teachers, I listen in to make sure we aren't putting the cart before the horse out of love for a particular resource. This happens a lot with what I call recycled lessons. As soon as you hear yourself say, "Here's what we used last year . . . ," stop and reflect. Just because it worked last year doesn't mean it's what this year's students need. In the same vein, when you plan, be careful to clarify the curricular goal first. This connects to relevant-versus-related instruction, discussed earlier. If you're choosing your resources out of preference or bias without cross-checking them to make sure they're directly relevant, you're likely putting the cart before the horse without even realizing it. To flexibly plan your scaffolds, confirm the learning objective and where your students are in relation to it *before* you ever start to choose materials and activities.

Be cautious as well about any bias you may have toward one resource over another. Are you using the same read-alouds every year? Do you teach the same inferring lesson every year? I'm not saying your preferences aren't effective. Instead, I'm encouraging you to be intentional when you use them. Ask yourself, "Even though I really like this activity (or resource), is it directly relevant to our learning objective, and does it meet the specific needs of my current learners?"

Another way we can practice flexibility with resources is by being more discriminatory about what we put in front of our learners. Over the years, we accumulate files and files of lesson ideas, resources, and techniques. And every year, we acquire even more. If you're like me, your filing cabinets are bursting at the seams with old favorites, and your desk is surrounded by new things you want to try. What's a teacher to do? Be selective! Both old and new resources can be valuable, and if they are, hang on to them. But don't keep using old resources just because you've had them forever, and don't embrace something as incredibly effective just because it's new. Be mindful and choosy. Always reflect on the quality of your resources and activities so that you can learn to be flexible in saying yes or no to them.

THINKING FLEXIBLY ABOUT GROUP SIZE

Not every learner will require the same amount or degree of support, so you'll also want to practice flexibility as you plan the size of the group you'll work with. Depending on your objective and your students, some scaffolds can be delivered effectively in whole-group lessons, others will lend themselves to smaller groups, and still others are better suited for individual instruction. Generally speaking, the smaller the group, the more effective your scaffolds will be, because you can target needs better and keep engagement higher, all while monitoring student responses more closely.

When you design your scaffolds, be open to the possibility that some objectives might require a deliberate shift in group size as you move through the scaffolding progression. For instance, you might model paragraphing with your whole class, and then pull back to work through the *share* and *support* portions of the scaffold with small groups. As the class moves closer and closer to independence, you'll likely notice a few students who need follow-up instruction and continue scaffolding their understanding of paragraphing individually. Again, flexibility is the key.

Depending on countless variables, scaffolding learners in the construction zone could appropriately happen in whole-class, individual, or small-group settings. As you look over Figure 4.1, notice how the 5S progression carries across the literacy block, affording various options for grouping learners.

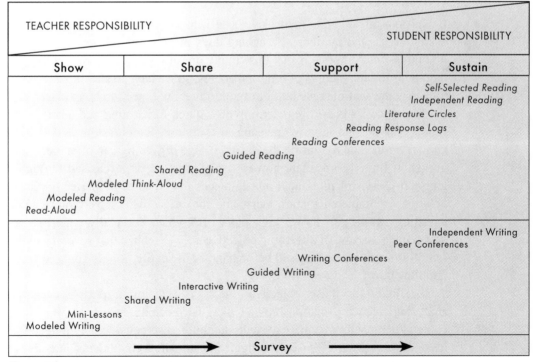

Figure 4.1
Progression of Responsibility Across the Literacy Block

How do you determine if something is best taught as a whole class, in a small group, or individually? To help you decide, you might consider the learning goal against the 80/50/10 approximation. This rough calculation helps you sort out who needs you most. Let's say Mrs. Garcia is concerned that her third graders aren't using ending marks effectively in their written compositions. If, after assessing the situation more closely, she realizes that around 80 percent of her students are struggling with it, she might consider bringing that scaffold to the whole group. If around 50 percent of them are having difficulty, she might consider working on this skill in small groups instead. And if, despite her original concerns, she finds that the numbers are actually closer to 10 percent, she would likely do well to scaffold this learning objective at the individual level.

It's vital to note that the 80/50/10 approximation isn't set in stone, and it isn't an absolute. It's simply a guide to help you think about how you'll plan certain scaffolds more effectively. I encourage you to practice flexibility with this rule of thumb as well.

THINKING FLEXIBLY ABOUT TIME

If you took all of your grade level's learning objectives and divided them evenly across the number of teaching days in your school year, one of the first things you'd notice is that this simply doesn't work. Different objectives require different amounts of time and energy, so we have to stay flexible about how long the scaffolds we build to support them will need to be in place.

Some scaffolds are short term, with a quick turnaround and a brief time stamp. Making the letter *a*, pausing at a comma for phrasing, and writing known words quickly during the drafting stage of writing can often be taught in a short time. More often, however, scaffolds are time released through a long-term series of integrated puzzle pieces that need to be perfectly placed before the completed picture can come into view. This may require some adjusting on our part as we kink out what's what, especially when we get down to the marrow of a learning objective only to realize that several smaller scaffolds need to be addressed beforehand or the entire thing's going to come tumbling down.

Scaffolds for these objectives, such as revising a draft for clarity, analyzing character relationships, or merging meaning, structure, and visual cuing systems with automaticity will, no doubt, take considerably longer. For instance, one group of teachers struggled to support their students' attempts at annotating texts while reading and realized that such a broad strategy would actually take several years to teach effectively. To accomplish this, each grade level took on a specific piece of the skill, adding cumulatively to the scaffold put in place by the previous grade level. Over time, their readers gained strengths in identifying important information while reading and jotting notes to preserve their thinking (Fisher and Frey 2012).

As you identify your instructional goals, think about how much time you'll need to accomplish them by making room for this difference between short- and long-term scaffolds. Then, consider these time frames against the needs of your learners and craft your scaffolds accordingly.

DECONSTRUCTING SCAFFOLDS

In addition to staying open minded about resources, group size, and time, you'll want to be flexible about how long your scaffolds will stay in place. Remember, scaffolds are designed to be temporary. They're not permanent structures. Instead, we progressively deconstruct them through each stage of the gradual release process. With every forward shift in the learner's degree of mastery, we take down a little bit more of the scaffold to align with this further, expanded level of his or her independence. As we eventually see evidence that the construction is completed and the student has mastered the objective completely, we remove the last of our supports and take down the scaffold entirely.

But when we lack intention about this deconstruction, we often leave our scaffolds in place for far too long, running the risk of students never learning to stand on their own. As a result, learners become either dependent or disinterested. At their worst, these perpetual scaffolds can end up hindering student progress. Think about a fourth grader who's still using finger pointing, an instructional support left over from years ago. Continuing this behavior (which has become habit) actually inhibits the child's phrasing, cadence, and speed. Since no one ever bothered to take the scaffold down, what was intended to help this student is having the opposite effect. When this happens, it can be incredibly difficult to get learners back on track.

Harvey Daniels (2002) speaks to this problem of keeping scaffolds in place long after their "sell-by" date has expired in the second edition of *Literature Circles*, in which he warns that the overuse of role sheets in book clubs and reading groups can actually backfire. When teachers forget their purpose and leave these brief, transitional supports in place too long, they inadvertently stifle the effects of their literature circles. With concern, Daniels writes, "What had been designed as a temporary support device to help peer-led discussion groups get started could actually undermine the activity it was meant to support" (13).

As you set out to design your scaffolds, practice flexibility around when you'll be taking them down. During the planning stages, create a plan for removal by asking yourself these questions:

- How will I know we're ready to move from one stage of the gradual release progression to the next? What signs will I look for?

- How will I know when it's time to pull back completely and release students to true independence? What evidence will I need?

The supports you put in place mustn't become permanent fixtures in your classroom. To that end, we have to ensure that the scaffolds we establish don't hang around too long and, in doing so, unintentionally jeopardize our work.

SCAFFOLD (N.) VERSUS SCAFFOLD (V.)

As you've been reading, you may have noticed that I have been using the word *scaffold* as both a verb and a noun, and at this point, I want to focus more specifically on scaffolds as a noun (n.). This is an important distinction to make. One is abstract, and the other is more concrete.

Scaffolding (v.) is something we *do* to move learners from point A to point B across the zone of proximal development—those decisive, intentional actions we take to guide students to independence. Scaffolds (n.), on the other hand, are the temporary tools, structures, and artifacts we put in place to help make that happen.

As you practice flexibility in your instructional design, you'll want to give some thought to these supports and how they can reinforce your teaching. For clarity, we'll organize our discussion of scaffolds (n.) around three learning modalities, which you'll likely find familiar:

auditory: scaffolds that students hear or say

kinesthetic: scaffolds that require touch or physical movement

visual: scaffolds that students see

The great news is that you probably already draw on these methods to periodically lend a hand when your children need it. No doubt you already use visuals around your room to help them work independently, and you're probably no stranger to providing concrete experiences with manipulatives or incorporating movement to engage your students physically.

Still, remembering that our aim is to increase our awareness about our instructional decisions, let's take a closer look at these tools and our intentions behind using them. As we do so, keep in mind that these three categories aren't exhaustive. For instance, supportive stories such as the silent *e* pinching a vowel to make it say its name or mnemonics such as editing with the acronym COPS (capitalization, organization, punctuation, and spelling) would certainly qualify as helpful scaffolds (n.) for many children even though they wouldn't fall neatly into the categories listed here. Even so, *auditory*, *kinesthetic*, and *visual* seem to exemplify the most prominent types of scaffolds, so we'll anchor our discussion with those.

AUDITORY SCAFFOLDS

In Texas, where I'm from, knowing how to two-step is almost expected. Unfortunately for me (and more than a few disgruntled dance partners along the way), I struggled for years to get this well-known dance step under my belt. Finally, a friend said, "Terry! It goes like this: slow, slow, quick, quick! Slow, slow, quick, quick!" After several more attempts with both of us repeating, "Slow, slow, quick, quick!" out loud, I finally got my bearings and could two-step with little effort. This was such a strong support for me that even after all these years, if I'm dancing to an unfamiliar tune, I'll find myself repeating in my head, *Slow, slow, quick, quick* until I can find the beat and get my footing. Auditory scaffolds (n.) such as chants like that one, verbal paths, familiar phrases, and even our instructional prompts and cues that call students to action can serve as small additions to your instructional efforts that have large implications.

In Chapter 2, we talked about focus phrases and how they can help us concentrate on the task at hand. But in addition to getting us started, we can give focus phrases new life as auditory scaffolds (n.), when we carry them beyond the introductory lesson and put them to work as ongoing reminders of important concepts we've taught before. For example, when I work with emergent writers, a focus phrase that frequently lingers as a continuing auditory scaffold (n.) as they're writing is "We use capitals only when we need them." Hearing this helps those few writers who still mix capital and lowercase letters remember that we usually write in lowercase letters—unless we have a good reason not to.

But auditory scaffolds can support learners far beyond memorable phrases. I recently helped a teacher whose beginning first graders struggled to grasp the campuswide voice-level expectations that range from silent to yelling. To support this, we came up with an auditory scaffold that had the added benefits of supporting fluency, left-to-right progression, sight words (*I, can, at, a*), and matching voice to text. During shared reading, the students practiced saying and hearing the nuances of voice level as they read the following chant from the sentence chart:

1. I can speak at a voice-level four!

2. I can speak at a voice-level three.

3. I can speak at a voice-level two.

4. I can speak at a voice-level one.

5. I can speak at a voice-level zero.

With each line of the chant, the group lowered their volume level just a bit to match its corresponding number. When they got to a voice-level zero (silence) they bobbed their heads as they read the words silently. In no time at all, the students grew accustomed to those voice-level ranges. A few days later, when their teacher reminded them that they were in the library and to use a voice-level one, everyone knew exactly what to do.

There are countless ways in which auditory scaffolds (n.) can help your students as they move closer and closer to independence (see Figure 4.2). Though these supports are initially heard as repeated outer conversations throughout the scaffolding (v.) process, they eventually become part of the inner conversation students take away when they work on their own.

KINESTHETIC SCAFFOLDS

Just as powerful as its auditory and visual counterparts but often less prominent in our instruction are physical, or kinesthetic, scaffolds. Anytime we bring movement or tactile interactions such as acting something out, using manipulatives, taking fine-motor actions to the gross-motor level, and

FOCUS	AUDITORY SCAFFOLD
Order of the alphabet	Singing—the classic ABC song
Letter formation	Verbal letter paths ("around, up, down, with a hook" to make a g)
Phrasing and cadence (fluency)	Echo reading—teacher models fluent reading, students repeat
Distinguishing between the two sounds of /oo/	Dramatically exaggerating an excited /oo/ and then a disgusted /oo/
Adding details to expository writing	Focus Phrase—"I include examples to support my central idea."
Reading for meaning	Reminders—"Remember when you read this to make sure it makes sense."
Monitoring and self-correcting	Prompts—"Read that again and see if you can find the mistake."

Figure 4.2
More Examples of Auditory Scaffolds

using hand gestures into the learning process, we encourage engagement while helping students more efficiently retain and retrieve what they need to be successful.

It seems we tend to remember physical scaffolds more with our youngest readers and writers. Think about it. We frequently use magnetic letters to support our word study efforts, and it isn't unusual for us to pull out a salt tray for kids to practice writing their word wall words or even take them outside to work on the pavement with sidewalk chalk. But our oldest kids can benefit from these types of scaffolds, too.

For instance, just before they went off to write after her mini-lesson, I watched a fourth-grade teacher lead her students through a quick round of "personal narrative yoga" designed to help them remember the different parts of the composition. The kids jumped to their feet and started stretching. Then, when everyone was ready, the teacher had the group reach high to the sky with their hands pressed together (for the beginning) and then move down, bending their knees while spreading their legs and widening their arms for the middle (since it's the largest part), and finally, squatting down and hugging their knees (for the conclusion). As they repeated the process several times, they breathed through each step, "Beginning, middle, and conclusion," in a voice that sounded for all the world like they were in the middle of an actual yoga session.

Teachers might scaffold upper-level students who are learning to attend to the conventions of nonfiction by giving them map pencils so they can physically box out nonfiction text features in different colors (such as title, graphics, bold print words, pictures, captions, and so on) as they read. Later in that same unit of study, readers might display one finger at time while enumerating the words *who*, *what*, *where*, *when*, and *why* as another physical scaffold (n.) to support them in identifying important details from the nonfiction text they're reading.

Physical scaffolds (n.) embody the meaning of new content while giving students a different experience with the information. They can be as elaborate as personal narrative yoga or as simple as clapping to hear syllables to spell larger words. Either way, inviting readers and writers to physically interact with tentative learning builds strong conduits to eventual independence. (Figure 4.3 provides even more examples of physical scaffolds.)

VISUAL SCAFFOLDS

In his best-selling book *Brain Rules*, molecular biologist John Medina (2008) discusses existing brain research and details ten insights about the way we think and learn. In rule number nine, he stresses that vision is "by far our most dominant sense, taking up half of our brain's resources" (240). In fact, Medina says, when learning something new, "the more visual the input becomes, the more likely it is to be recognized—and to be recalled" (233). The old saying that a picture is worth a thousand words definitely rings true here, and the savvy teacher can cash in on this notion by making use of constructive, well-chosen visual scaffolds (n.) to support students as they take on higher degrees of independence.

Even if they're simple, visuals can pack a powerful instructional punch. They're easily incorporated into your teaching, and you'll find plenty of options for displaying them prominently to bolster independence such as these:

FOCUS	PHYSICAL SCAFFOLD
Letter formation—*h*	Walking a giant chalk letter *h* on the sidewalk while repeating the formation path—"Down, down, down, and back up with a hump"
Hearing sounds across words	Pushing bingo chips as you listen for the individual sounds in order—/s/..../p/.../ar/.../k/
Left-to-right progression with a return sweep	Inviting the student to hold the pointer with you as you read through several lines of a big book together
Matching voice to print	Having the reader place his or her finger on top of yours as you touch each word
Identifying the difference between a letter and a word	Assigning students large letter cards and guiding them in rearranging themselves to make words by scrunching shoulder to shoulder while holding their letter cards up. (For example, "Who has the letter *a* and who has the letter *t*? You two come stand really, really close together. We're going to make the word *at*.")
Inferring	Repeating a motion from hands displayed out like a book to pointing to the brain to highlight that inferences are derived from merging what we read in text with what we're thinking in our minds
Spacing between words	Having students use their opposite thumb to "hold the space" as they start to write the next word
Vocabulary	Acting out the meaning of words (e.g., with *evaporation*, waving hands up from the ground to the sky and then, for *condensation* making a rumbly cloud by twisting their hands together high above their heads, and finally for *precipitation*, "raining" hands down from the sky to the ground)

Figure 4.3
More Examples of Physical Scaffolds

- **Prompting cards**—taped to desk, held in hand, or laid out on workspace

- **Table tents**—specifically designed to be displayed for small groups

- **Sticky notes**—posted inside books or notebooks for easy reference

- **Flap cards**—taped on the back cover of a notebook and flipped out as students are writing

- **Bookmarks**—tucked into books or just beside them

- **Anchor charts**—posted throughout the room

- **Wall displays**—whole areas available for students to use as a reference while learning (for example, word walls)

For instance, some of your learners may need a revising flap card like the one in Figure 4.4, a small group may need a cuing system table tent for what to do when they get stuck while reading (Figure 4.5), and still others may require a bookmark that reminds them of the elements to attend to when preparing to retell a narrative story (Figure 4.6). Even our first graders working on voice levels found a higher degree of support when their teacher added pictures to their sentence chart that ranged from a roaring lion for a level four to a silent turtle for a level zero.

Teachers Marjorie Martinelli and Kristine Mraz develop this concept a bit more deeply in their book *Smarter Charts* (2012). Taking a cue from the pioneering preschool approach of Reggio Emilia, they remind us that the visuals we use in our classrooms can serve as the "third teacher in the room" (xii), with visible representations of content, skills, and strategies. Essentially, as we gradually release students to increasing levels of responsibility, the visual scaffolds we provide can function as reference points until they can stand on their own.

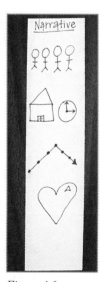

Figure 4.4
Revising Flap Card

Figure 4.5
Cuing System Table Tent

Figure 4.6
Retelling Bookmark

Recently, our fifth-grade team took advantage of this notion to support a series of lessons that would eventually culminate with their students both writing and identifying effective summaries of biographies. To clarify their focus, they first took some time to list the important elements in a strong biography summary:

1. The person develops over time.

2. The person is usually known for something important.

3. Events are generally discussed chronologically.

4. Major events in the person's life are highlighted.

5. A lesson, moral, or theme is often present.

Once these elements were identified, the teachers created memorable icons to represent them. To show that a person develops and grows over time, they drew a stick figure with an arrow pointing to a larger one. They used an exclamation mark to represent the person being known for something important and then sketched a beaded arrow to show chronological progression. A descending series of stars highlighted the major events in the person's life, and finally, they included a heart to remind students to look for a lesson, moral, or theme.

The team hit a snag at one point and had to think flexibly. In working with their students, they realized that they'd forgotten to include an important element in biographies: what was going on in the world around the person at the time. For instance, part of what makes Amelia Earhart important enough to write a biography about is the state of aviation in her world and the diminished role of female pilots in that history. Redoubling their efforts, the teachers added an icon—a small Earth—and crafted a few lessons to make room for that element.

With visuals at the ready, they presented each factor individually in its own series of lessons. In these discussions, they introduced the element's icon and used it as a visual scaffold to anchor various lessons on attending to its importance and making inferences around it. After each element was thoroughly explored, its icon was added to a cumulative anchor chart titled What's Important in a Biography (see Figure 4.7).

Finally, after establishing these components successfully, the classes turned their attention to using them to craft summaries. At this point, the children could easily identify these six building blocks of a biography and even quickly sketch out their correlating icons. Explaining that a strong summary would include information from all these elements, the teachers set about modeling and practicing using their visual reminders to summarize biographies with their students. To emphasize that summaries are brief but packed with information, they added an icon of a piece of candy as a comical reminder that summaries are short and sweet.

As students moved to working with groups and eventually on their own, they were encouraged to refer to the icons along the way if they needed help. To support this, they were given bookmarks with the six icons on them, and their note-taking pages included the visuals as well (see Figure 4.8a and 4.8b). The students even used the icons and anchor charts to scaffold their correlating research assignments where they had to study a famous person and write an end-of-unit biography, which then culminated in a multimedia presentation project.

Eventually, the children were summarizing the important elements of biographies independently without relying on having the visual scaffolds right beside them. Later, when the students were called on to identify strong summaries of biographical texts in test settings, their teachers returned to those familiar icons as a scaffold for them to refer to when learning to evaluate the effectiveness of each of the four multiple-choice answers.

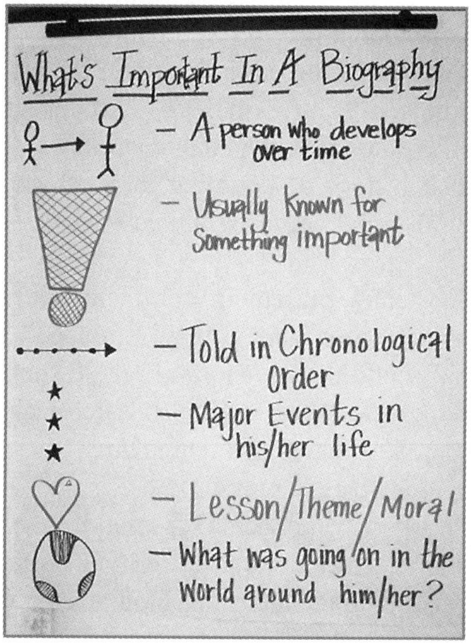

Figure 4.7
Cumulative Anchor Chart:
What's Important in a
Biography

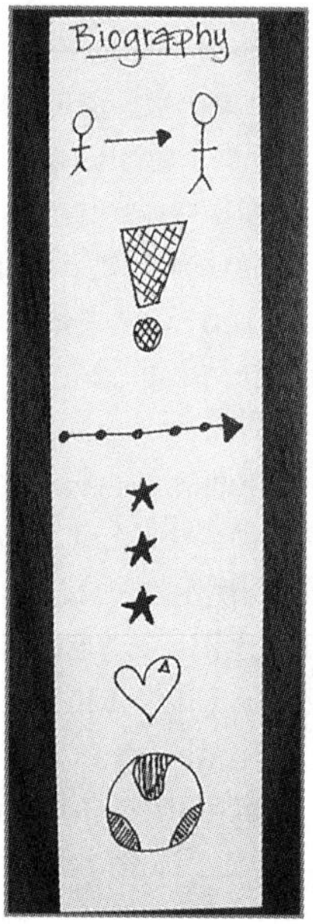

Figure 4.8a
Bookmark: What's
Important in a Biography

Summarizing a Biography

Name: _Cole . H_   Person I'm Studying: _Abraham lincoln_

♀→♀	He started out poor, but ended up president.	★★★	- became president - Won the civil war - Kept north and South together - Freed slaves - was shot and killed
❗	He was the 16th president he freeded slaves	♡	you need to stand up for what is right
•••►	Abe lincoln grew up in a log cabin. He became a lawyer then he was a congressman. He became an Important president.	🌍	Slavery Civil war
🍬	REMEMBER – When you write a summary, include these elements but keep it short and sweet!		

Figure 4.8b
Note-taking Page: What's Important in a Biography

The readers in this example were eventually able to write, identify, and summarize biographies successfully because their teachers planned specific visual supports to enhance their instruction. Whether they're crafted for whole-class instruction or personalized for individual needs, using images in this way can offer immediate scaffolds (n.) that remind readers and writers of the skills they're learning as they go off to try them on their own. Figure 4.9 provides more examples of visual scaffolds.

FOCUS	VISUAL SCAFFOLD
Appropriate spacing when writing	Using your eraser to gauge spaces between your words and your pencil tip to gauge spaces between your letters
Revising for clarity in writing	Modeling—"Watch me while I reread what I've written and circle the parts that don't quite make sense yet."
Fluent phrasing	Pause breaks marked into the text—quick pause for one slash and a full stop for two (e.g., "After we were finished,/ we went to the pool/ to pick up my sister.//")
Nonfiction text structures	Anchor chart with ✓ Lock and Key = problem and solution; ✓ Cloud and Umbrella = cause and effect; ✓ Venn Circles = comparison; ✓ Ladder = sequential steps; ✓ Art Palate = descriptive; and ✓ Numbered Bullets = list
Genres	Cumulative genre bulletin board with reduced-size photocopies of book covers and articles the class has read so far this year sorted into appropriate genres
Independent reading expectations	Stoplight bookmarks with different degrees of expectations for independent reading time (e.g., green—"I think hard about my reading most of the time," yellow—"I lose my focus a few times, but I can get back on track," red—"I fake read most of the time and forget to pay attention").
Adding details to personal narratives	Flap card that folds up from the back cover of writing notebooks with ✓ a heart for bringing in feelings, ✓ an art brush and framed painting for adding vivid details, ✓ a running stick figure for including actions, ✓ a thought bubble for sharing thinking, and ✓ a speech bubble for incorporating dialogue
Narrative text structures	Bookmark with ✓ Stick Figures = characters; ✓ House and Clock = setting (time and place); ✓ Numbered Plot Arc = plot in sequence; and ✓ Heart = theme, moral, or lesson

Figure 4.9
More Examples of Visual Scaffolds

MERGING SCAFFOLDS

Though we've explored them individually, you'll notice that scaffolds (n.) frequently overlap. This is because several scaffolds (n.) working in tandem to reach more than one learning style can be considerably more effective (see Figure 4.10). Depending on the needs of your learners, you'll want to make clear decisions about the levels and different types of supports they'll need. For instance, we might have kindergarten writers practicing the letter *g*, making the letter as large as they can in a salt tray (kinesthetic) while at the same time saying out loud, "Around, up, down, down, down, with a hook" (auditory) and then comparing their attempt with the letter printed on a card next to the salt tray (visual). When you use more than one type of scaffold, you'll reach students with multiple techniques that can have a synergistic effect on the way they take on new knowledge.

At this point, we circle back to familiar principles woven throughout this book: intentionality and reflection. Remember, everything we do instructionally must have a purpose that's tied directly to a focus stemming from what our students need to move forward. Practice purposefulness with your scaffolds (n.) as well. Not every skill or every student will require the same level of support. When well-meaning educators demand that an anchor chart accompany every lesson, for instance, we defeat the purpose of this type of scaffold. Again, flexibility is the key.

In this same breath, it bears reiterating that scaffolds (n.) are gradually released. They're intended to be around for only a short time. As soon as your observations show that your children no longer need their support, start the removal process. For instance, once the skill is mastered, a writer can stop repeating, "Down, down, down, and back up with a hump" to make a letter *h*. And though it makes perfect sense to remind a child that he or she no longer needs to speak the verbal path of the letter *h*, other removals may be less obvious. Think about our fifth graders summarizing biographies. When should their visual scaffolds come down? This can get tricky. Some readers will need those supports in place a bit longer, and a few will be ready to work without them fairly quickly. Others may need to return to them only periodically when they get in a bind (remember my auditory scaffold: slow, slow, quick, quick).

GOAL/FOCUS	AUDITORY SCAFFOLD	VISUAL SCAFFOLD	PHYSICAL SCAFFOLD
1:1 Matching	"Make it match."	Dots under words—placed temporarily to show students where to finger point under the word	Cut sentence and spread it out along the floor so students can frog jump as they read each of the words.
Sight word *the*	Chant: "You can say /thuh/ or you can say /the/—but either way you spell it, it's T-H-E."	Teacher points to the word *the* and its individual letters on the board during the chant	When children get to the part of the chant where they spell *the*, they motion arms out (for *t*), arms high (for *h*), and arms around their knees (for *e*).
Reading left to right across words	"Run the bases in order."	Table card with dot arrow under words	Write the word in large letters on whiteboard so readers use gross-motor skills to finger slide across the words.
Fluent phrasing	Echo reading—teacher models fluent reading of a line and students mimic teacher's inflection, pauses, and stops	Pause breaks—quick pause for one slash and full stop for two (e.g., "After we were finished,/ we went to the pool/ to pick up my sister.//")	With hands outstretched (like they're holding handlebars) read aloud from sentence chart while pretending they're slowing to turn a corner at a comma, and rocking back at a period for a full stop.

Figure 4.10
Merging Scaffolds (n.)

The various answers to this question spring directly from how you'll decisively respond to the multiple needs in your classroom.

Despite that, I can give you at least one absolute answer to the question "How long should this scaffold stay in place?" Not indefinitely. Just as we reduce the intensity of our scaffolding (v.) as learners gain mastery, we gradually remove our scaffolds (n.) as they gain proficiency. Eventually, when they're no longer needed, anchor charts and table tents come down, songs and chants are forgotten, and the manipulatives get put away. They've served their purpose well, and we were glad to have them for a time, but they're no longer needed.

CONSTRUCTIVE REFLECTIONS

1. Think of a concept you teach the same way year after year. Are you working from an absolute mind-set? Could it be taught differently? More effectively? Are there other options?

2. When you sit down to plan (alone or with your peers), what's the first thing you look at? The standard? Your resources? Where your students are in relation to the goal? How does the order in which you reflect on these make a difference in the way you design your scaffolds?

3. How do you decide what will be taught in whole group, in small group, or on an individual level? What are your intentional practices with this decision?

4. Think of a skill or strategy your students struggle to master. Is there a different way you could teach it? Are there some other methods you might try? What effect might these changes have on the way your learners attend to and incorporate this new material?

5. Reflect on a concept you find difficult to teach. Brainstorm some auditory, physical, or visual scaffolds you haven't tried yet. How could they support your efforts and your students' independence?

6. Often, scaffolds are unintentionally left to die on the vine (for example, finger pointing for one-to-one matching, getting your mouth ready for initial-sound visual cuing, story maps for retelling). What are some scaffolds (n.) that you might tend to leave around too long? For instance, when does an anchor chart in your room come down? How do you know it's time? What process do you go through to make that decision?

CHAPTER 5 FLEXIBLE DELIVERY:
MONITORING PROGRESS AND MAKING ADJUSTMENTS

So. You've covered all your bases. You've taken the time to clarify your focus, you've given serious thought to where your students are, and you've planned deliberate lessons to get them where they need to be. You're ready.

But what if you're wrong?

Within the first eight hours of your teaching career, you probably discovered one of Murphy's Laws that still haunts you even today: sometimes, despite our best efforts, the lessons we've planned so intentionally don't quite go the way we'd anticipated. This difference between what we intended and the reality of how the scaffold unfolds often calls for adjustments on our part, demanding flexibility in the ways we support our students.

In addition to intentional planning, scaffolding involves our calculated responses to the ways our students react to the instruction we provide. If something isn't working or if learners need more (or less) assistance, we counter by shifting our levels of support up or down as our scaffold moves closer and closer to its intended target. In this way, scaffolding is alive and organic. It builds on itself, replenishes itself, flexes, and regroups—all in the moment. Our teaching expands or contracts responsively to meet the needs of the students in front of us.

In effect, we adjust our instructional arrow in midflight.

This flexible, responsive quality is an integral element of scaffolding. But proceed with caution here; there's a significant difference between being responsive and veering completely off course. Yes, scaffolding is adaptable, and we're open to bending and shifting as needs arise throughout the gradual release progression, but we make these adjustments while remaining consciously aware of the intentions behind everything we do in the construction zone. We can revise our well-laid plans—and even desert them if it comes to that—but we do so with good reasons. As you move through this chapter, remember: *flexibility doesn't mean random or haphazard.*

As with every other aspect of instructional scaffolding, flexibility is intentional.

SURVEYING AND FLEXIBILITY

Staying flexible as we move through the instructional process can be difficult, especially when we're caught off guard or aren't quite sure what to do. Moving from designing lessons grounded in the gradual release progression to delivering instruction that modifies itself within and from that same process takes an open mind and a keen eye. Recall that one of the major advantages of emphasizing the gradual release model through the 5S progression is that it allows us to highlight the importance of ongoing assessment through the fifth S—survey. To survey means to be in continual observation, collecting evidence and gathering data throughout the progression from showing, to sharing, to supporting and sustaining.

With this in mind, the first step in flexible teaching is to remain in a constant mind-set of assessment—observing, considering, and evaluating. This is crucial. As educational researcher and scholar Nell Duke (2011) reminds us, "A knowledgeable teacher who observes students carefully is our best tool." Effective scaffolders are kid watchers. They ask questions. They interact closely with students, getting to know them as individuals and as learners. They're watchful. They're aware. They notice everything.

And, as they're watching and noticing, they're asking themselves a critical question: "Do I stay the course or do I need to make some adjustments?" If everything is going well, it makes perfect sense to stay the course. If not, then you'll need to make some changes.

This may sound easier than it really is. Though it's unintentional on our part, many of us are more resistant to making instructional adjustments than we like to think. Sometimes we're so set on our plans working that we dig our heels in and stay the course regardless, all the while hoping our students will eventually fall in line. If you've tried this option, you know how well it works—or, rather, doesn't work. Staying the course despite and beyond evidence that tells you something isn't working is ill advised and only frustrates our learners while robbing them of precious learning time they really don't have to spare.

If it comes to it, be prepared to completely jettison your plan and make a new one. Yes, this can be difficult. When we've spent so much energy crafting a lesson only to watch it go up in flames right in front of our eyes, it can be really hard to let it go. But sometimes, despite any reluctance and disappointment on our part, it really is best to throw the plan out the window, head back to the drawing board (with a giant bag of chocolate!), and make a new plan. If you find this happening to you more frequently than you'd like, take some time for reflection and figure out why. Ask yourself these questions:

- Does my instructional plan have a clearly defined focus?

- Is my focus overestimating (or underestimating) the zone of proximal development?

- Does my focus have smaller, incremental objectives that need to be addressed before my learners can take this one on?

- Are my focus and instructional plan based in student assessment?

More often, though, you'll notice that your plan isn't so much completely mistaken as it is off by a degree or two. In this case, finding your way becomes a matter of taking a good look at your instruction, your focus, and the evidence you've gathered through observing your students. Pinpoint the part where things went wrong, and make adjustments to get back on track.

LEARNING TO TRUST YOUR GUT

Reflection is the backbone of intentionality, but to be reflective, we first have to be watchful. Just like our fifth-grade teachers in the previous chapter who—through the course of their biography planning—realized they'd failed to include the important biographical element of what was going on in the world around the person and quickly shifted their instruction to make room for it, observant teachers are always on the lookout for when their plans need some adjusting. Scaffolding with a mind-set of assessment depends largely on our ability to slow things down so we can clear our minds and take the time required to simply watch.

But even after we've done this, many of us still lack confidence in our own perceptions. This was one of the hardest lessons I had to learn when I started out. I used to get so frustrated waiting for a straight answer from my teacher leader, who, no matter how much I insisted, always pushed me to defend my observations and justify my own thinking. She wouldn't do it for me. Don't get me wrong: I'm sure she understood that a part of learning is seeking confirmation of our thinking, but it was more than that—and she saw what I couldn't. I didn't trust my intuition. And because I didn't trust it, I couldn't act on it to make those in-the-moment shifts necessary to fortify my scaffolding.

That was years ago. These days, I'm on the other side of the conversation, as the teachers I work with approach me to look at data they've collected or share an anecdote about a teaching scenario that has them puzzled. As a literacy coach, my first attempt is to steer them toward drawing their own conclusions just like my teacher leader did so well for me. "What do you notice?" I ask. And even though they get just as frustrated as I did back in the day, more often than not, their responses confirm that they've had their answers all along. They just didn't trust what they were seeing.

Beneath all its technical details, scaffolding is an intuitive process. Think about the classic scaffolding experience of parents teaching their children to walk. They don't wait for confirmation from someone else to validate their instincts about when and how to do it. Most of what they know to do comes from careful noticing and instinctive responding. In the same way, flexible instruction depends on the teacher as a keen observer who naturally looks for cues and then confidently acts on that evidence.

As an observant, more knowing other in the scaffolding process, we have an internal barometer, a sort of instinct that looks to student responses as indicators to help us recalibrate our next steps. Sometimes it materializes as a gut feeling, a nagging notion, or an intuitive impression. Other times, it crops up as a dawning awareness. And, every now and then it surprises us in a flash of insight. But we all have one.

Trust yours.

LOOKING CLOSELY AND MAKING ADJUSTMENTS

An essential quality of responsive teaching is remaining in awareness so you can monitor how things are going, how your teaching is working, and how your students are responding (or not responding) to it. Along the way, you'll have lots of important decisions to make, and being observant will keep you one step ahead, so you can see most of the curve balls in plenty of time to do something about them.

Flexible delivery, then, means adjusting our scaffolds as our understanding of our students' needs becomes clearer.

Knowing the right instructional changes to make and when to make them—all while you're in the middle of teaching—is a skill that can take years to master. Still, you can refine this decision-making process by checking it against information about your *learner*, your *focus*, and your *instruction*. New information about any of these three elements could cause your entire scaffold to shift, and if it does, you'll want to be ready.

- *Learner:* evidence you've gathered through observation about the student's needs—including strengths, weaknesses, and responses to your instruction

- *Focus:* the goal, what you want the learner to eventually control independently

- *Instruction:* your ongoing plan, practices, and delivery as you scaffold the learner to the next level

For a more concrete illustration, imagine that these factors (learner, focus, and instruction) are the three points of a flexible, equilateral triangle (see Figure 5.1) and your task is to keep them as aligned as possible. As you work

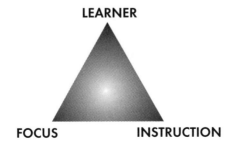

LEARNER

FOCUS   **INSTRUCTION**

Figure 5.1
The Flexible Delivery Triangle

through the gradual release progression, plenty of obstacles and unexpected turns will cause your triangle to shift. And, each of those shifts will require different decisions and actions on your part to keep your scaffolding balanced.

For instance, say you realize that your instruction is out of sync with your objective or simply isn't meeting your children's needs. In that case, you'd shift your teaching to bring it back into line with your focus and your learners.

In the same way an entire mobile sways if you hit one of its parts, each individual element of the triangle (learner, focus, instruction) can affect the others if it gets out of whack. Don't let this throw you. If you're watching for it, you'll be able to pinpoint exactly where you need to go to make your adjustments.

LEARNER

Notice that the learner is in a paramount spot at the top of our triangle. This signifies the important role that our students and their data play in the scaffolding process. Unlike the other two points of your scaffolding triangle, which you can adapt based on new information, your learner's needs and performance aren't something over which you have direct control. You can influence them, but you can't dictate them. As you move through the scaffolding process, your students constantly take on new learning. They're changing right before your eyes, and you'll want to pay close attention to even the slightest shifts in what they control, so you can adjust your instruction or objective accordingly. In essence, what you'll teach tomorrow depends on what you see your learners control today.

When we continually survey our students' responses to our instruction, we look for patterns and for evidence that reveals what they know as well as where they're uncertain. What's more, effective scaffolders gather data from as many sources as possible. Numerous opportunities to watch kids, such as visiting one-on-one during reading and writing conferences, looking over writing samples, analyzing running records, watching students work, listening in on their small-group discussions, or even grading their pencil-and-paper attempts—all offer information that can inform our decisions about the next, right steps to move our scaffolds along. But even then, all that data could be worthless if we don't know exactly what we're looking for.

Late one fall, a new first-grade teacher stopped me in the hall and said she was worried about a group of students who didn't know their letter names and sounds yet. She was concerned because we were inching up on the winter break and they weren't making the progress she'd hoped for. "We've been over and over this," she said, "but I have three kids who still don't know their letters and sounds."

"What do you mean?" I asked, encouraging her to dig deeper. "They don't know *any* of their letters and sounds or they know only a *few*?" We had a quick conversation in which we revisited the importance of using data (survey) to zero in on a precise problem and decided we needed more information. "Let's meet up tomorrow with your assessment notes for each kiddo and see if I can help you figure out what's going on," I said.

During our meeting the next day, we looked over an observation sheet with the following data she'd collected (Figure 5.2).

As you look over her data, what do you notice? Look closely.

	Student 1	Student 2	Student 3
Letter Names	b for d (but self-corrects it) L for *I* (but self-corrects it)	W for M (but self-corrects it)	i for *l* (but self-corrects it)
Letter Sounds	/y/ for u /k/ for q /w/ for y /ch/ for h /j/ for g	/y/ for u /d/ for w /s/ for c /j/ for g	/j/ for g /y/ for u /s/ for c /ay/ for h

Figure 5.2
Using Precise Data to Zero In On Students' Letter Learning

Making instructional adjustments depends on knowing what to look for during the scaffolding process. But finding a sense of direction while digging through charts full of data—or more often, while you're in the middle of teaching—can be overwhelming. To help with this, I encourage teachers to focus their observations by reflecting on three practical, guiding questions:

- Are they getting it?

- Are they almost getting it?

- Where will we need to go next?

As you get used to asking these questions, you'll soon notice that they work in tandem throughout the scaffolding process. This is especially true when you use them to guide your in-the-moment observations and reflections. For instance, say I'm in the middle of teaching students in a third-grade writing workshop the craft of tagging character actions to dialogue. (For example, "'Get out of here!' she yelled, scowling and pointing her finger at the doorway.") While I'm watching kids write, conferring with them individually, and reading over their efforts, I'm going to be in a continual mind-set of assessment, pinging back and forth among these questions simultaneously and wondering, "Did they get it? Are they close to getting it?" and "In light of this, where might our scaffold need to take them next?"

Now let's consider these guiding questions as we look at the notes presented in Figure 5.2. As simplistic as this data may look at first glance, it holds quite a bit of valuable information about these first graders, where they are with their letters and sounds, and where they need to go next.

Are they getting it?

This question is about reality and evidence. When we ask whether they're getting it, we're looking to see if our observations prove that our learners have met or at least are on course to meet the objective. Holding these results up to the original objective their teacher had set in place (knowing all their letter names and sounds), we start to see that these first graders are approaching the target even if they're not hitting it 100 percent of the time yet. Through our survey efforts, we can tell that it isn't so much that they don't know their letters and sounds as we'd originally assumed. They actually know quite a few of them. They just seem to have some lingering confusions that need to be shored up.

Are they almost getting it?

Effective scaffolders keep an eye out for approximations. When you look at Figure 5.2, ask yourself, "What evidence do we have that these three youngsters *almost* know their letters and sounds?" This question is about looking specifically at the errors we see. Errors and approximations can be incredibly useful in the scaffolding process, because they're a window into what kids are thinking. When we look closely at the observation data, we notice how the first graders are confusing the names of visually similar letters (such as *b* for *d* and *W* for *M*)—but only to a degree, because they seem aware of this confusion to the point that they're consistently monitoring for it and self-correcting it. This tells us that they're well on their way with their letter names.

When we look specifically at their letter sound errors, a clear pattern emerges. Notice how this group struggles with letters that don't make the sound of their names like most other letters do. Think about it—*u* doesn't make the /y/ sound its name begins with, *w* doesn't start with /d/ like it should, and worst of all, the letter *h* doesn't go /ay/ or /ch/! Can you imagine how confusing this can be to these early readers? But they're close, aren't they? Their approximations tell us that this group of first graders just hasn't figured out yet what many of their peers learned much earlier: some letters don't make the sound of their names.

Where will we need to go next?

In her book *Learning for Keeps*, staff developer Rhoda Koenig (2010) reminds us, "When students experience confusion, when they have difficulty constructing meaning from text, when their writing fails to communicate clearly, when they are unable to solve problems, teachers use their observations to plan and provide mediation" (5). While we're teaching, we're constantly weighing what our learners need next in light of what we're observing. This notion is the heart of flexible delivery. It's about possibilities.

As we uncovered their error patterns, I'm sure your internal lightbulb was glowing as you simultaneously started thinking about next steps for these first graders. When we look specifically at letter names (not sounds) for these children, it seems advisable to stay the course. They know almost all of them, and they seem fully aware of the names they're hesitant with. It looks like they just need more time for their tentative knowing to solidify. We could probably support this best by naming and affirming the effective monitoring and self-correcting they're already doing.

But what about those letter sounds? Where would we go next? It does seem like some slight recalibration might be in order. Perhaps it's time to reteach these sounds with a heavier focus on the idea that some letters don't make the sound of their names and doing so with a specific attention to this handful of rule breakers.

Being a kid watcher (survey) involves knowing what to look for, developing trust in your perceptions, and confidently acting on them. Holding these guiding questions in your mind as you work will help you keep your eyes and ears open for new or unexpected evidence that can guide you to better decisions and adjustments in your teaching. This vigilance is our fundamental function as a more knowing other, and flexible delivery in our scaffolding depends on it.

FOCUS

Even if you've worked hard to put a strong focus in place, be open to changing your instructional goal if you need to. This corner of the flexible delivery triangle ties directly to monitoring student needs. If the objective is too easy or if learners progress quickly, be prepared to move your focus forward earlier than planned.

However, more commonly, a lack of student progress may indicate that your focus is too hard for now and a slightly different objective is in order. We often discover a misaligned goal when we try to push learners to perform outside their zone of proximal development. Remember, if the goal is too hard, students get frustrated and shut down. If that's the case, shifting to a more appropriate objective will help you sort things out.

Remember our earlier discussion of the difference between related and relevant instruction in Chapter 2? This is another common area where our focus can get distorted, requiring some adjustments on our part. Unfortunately, it's often so slight that many of us overlook it. Last year, Jennifer called me in to observe her work with her third graders, who had missed several inferring questions on their fall benchmark assessments. "I don't get it," she said. "We've been working on inferring for a while, and when we're talking about texts, their inferences seem dead-on. But they still got way too many of these questions wrong."

Later, a quick look at my observation notes and her collected data revealed the trouble. She was right: her kids could infer quite well. If they were asked how a character felt, for instance, they could tell you exactly. The problem was that they weren't accustomed to justifying where their inferences came from. When the question said, "What from the story shows the reader that Cindy felt excited at the party?" they agreed she was excited but weren't always quite sure how to respond. Armed with this new understanding, Jennifer changed her scaffolding focus from naming inferences and instead crafted a series of lessons with a new, directly relevant objective: supporting inferences using text evidence.

Being open to adapting your focus will prepare you for setbacks you might otherwise miss because the objective you're working on blinds you to other, more effective possibilities. You can zero in on possible adjustments in your focus by asking yourself these questions:

- Is it possible that I'm in the middle of a relevant-versus-related focus confusion?

- Is this goal within my students' proximal level of learning?

- Have my learners mastered any smaller, incremental goals that need to be met first?

- Do my observations show me that my students are ready to take on more?

- Is my evidence showing me that I need to shift the degree of difficulty down?

In the end, whether you've set the focus yourself or are working through a state or district expectation, stay vigilant about whether the goal is right for your students and their needs. If you find that your focus is misaligned, it's time to consider some changes that will bring your triangle back into balance.

INSTRUCTION

When your focus is clear and you're working in a continual mind-set of assessment, the part of the triangle with the most room to flex is the third point: your instruction. Since you have the most control over this element, it's up to you to monitor your teaching for effectiveness and any adjustments that need to be made. Being the more knowing other doesn't mean you know everything. If something in your scaffold feels off, double back and take a hard look at your instructional plan and practices, and see if you need to make some decisive changes.

For instance, if at some stage in the scaffolding process your observations indicate that your student's needs were originally misinterpreted or they've shifted in some way, and assuming your focus stays the same, you'd shift your instructional plan to bring things into alignment.

To support this self-monitoring, consider recording yourself from time to time or have a trusted peer observe your scaffolding efforts and give you feedback. This can be especially helpful when you know something is off in your scaffolding but can't seem to pinpoint the exact problem. Years ago, I struggled with a group of disinterested fifth-grade readers who slumped across the table with their heads in their hands, completely passive about what we were doing. When I watched a video of one of our lessons, I was mortified to see that I was slouching just as badly! It turned out that I was modeling with my behaviors the exact thing I was trying to get them to stop doing. You can bet I fixed that immediately.

But still, this was a good reminder that as a more knowing other, our decisions, words, and even our actions set the tone for and drive our scaffolds. Regardless of how you do it, take note of these details and how your kids are responding to them during the scaffolding process. If you notice that something you're doing, saying, or planning isn't supporting them in just the right way, get in there and make some changes. To help with this, let's consider several significant areas where you might make instructional shifts to effectively redirect the course of your scaffolds.

CONSIDER SHIFTING STAGES IN THE GRADUAL RELEASE

Certainly, some of your scaffolds will proceed sequentially from *showing* to *sharing* to *supporting* and finally to *sustaining*. But this generally isn't the case. In most scaffolding scenarios, things are recursive and can feel more like a bob and weave than a direct advance. A large part of flexing your instruction from and within the gradual release progression is acknowledging that the process isn't always linear. In real life, things tend to go back and forth, in and out, and anywhere in between.

At any time, your learners' responses could point you in a new direction. Your observations may tell you they're ready to move on to the next stage, stay put for a bit, or repeat a previous stage. At times, your kid watching may even tell you it would be best to go all the way back to modeling and start over. As each step in the process occurs, your learners are taking on more and more independence. This is your indicator. Be looking for it. As students show you what they can do, be ready to shift your teaching further up or down the progression. Remember, even though our scaffolds are rooted in the gradual release progression, we can expect some branching out along the way.

Beyond adjustments you'll make for higher and lower degrees of independence, be on the lookout for the stages that will require more attention than the others. For instance, teaching your third graders to summarize nonfiction might take considerably more modeling (show) than it took to teach them to retell fiction.

With this in mind, stay aware of stages you tend to neglect or unintentionally give more effort to. This varies with individual teachers. Some of us lean too heavily on modeling, whereas others forget the importance of taking the time to ensure that learners see explicit examples before moving on to trying a new skill. One grade-level team I planned with over a series of months noticed that, though they modeled (show) instruction well, things often fell apart when their kids went off to work independently (sustain). After several struggles with this pattern, the team finally realized that they weren't dedicating enough instructional real estate to the shared part of scaffolding. They aren't alone. Lots of teachers struggle with this. In my experience, the "we do" portion of the scaffolding progression seems to be the most overlooked. This is unfortunate, because sharing and supporting is where the majority of our scaffolding takes place. Kids need lots of practice with most new learning before they can master it. If you've modeled something really well, but your kids don't seem to be transferring it to their independent work, the culprit may be a lack of time spent sharing the load with them. Go back and spend more energy revisiting the sharing and supporting stages of the 5S progression, and you'll likely see a considerable change.

Keeping the following guiding questions in mind when you plan and while you teach will help keep you aware of where you are and where you need to be in the scaffolding progression:

- Considering my focus and my learner's needs, which stages of the progression will I need to give greater attention to?

- Am I personally biased more toward any of the stages?

- Have I intentionally planned for each stage, keeping in mind how each will support my learners' movement toward independence?

- Where are we in the 5S progression? Am I looking for evidence from my learners to help me decide when it's time to shift to the next stage?

- How flexible am I about the amount of time I plan to stay at each stage?

That last question brings us back to timing issues. As you're working through the scaffolding stages, be mindful of how long you'll stay in each one and be open to changing if you need to. Even if you start out with a good idea of how things will go and you've thought about how much energy each stage is likely to require, your learners' responses will tell you if they need to move faster or slower through the progression.

CONSIDER CHANGING TEACHER TO STUDENT RATIO

Another change you might consider is how your group configuration (whole group, small group, individual) can support your movement through the gradual release progression. In Chapter 4, when we reviewed this concept, we were looking specifically at the planning stages of our scaffolds. But keep in mind that increasing or decreasing the size of your learning group is also the type of decision you can make or remake *during* the instructional process. As you're teaching, ask yourself, "What group size would fit this part of the progression best?"

It's easy to forget that group size doesn't have to stay the same throughout the whole scaffolding process. Just because you start out working in a large group doesn't mean you can't shift to smaller groups if it would serve your purpose better. This can swing in the other direction, too. I once decided to move a small-group kindergarten phonemic awareness lesson to a whole-class

class because the group was having difficulty, and I wanted them to have the benefit of hearing their stronger peers model taking apart the sounds of words.

You might even find it useful to shift to different group sizes as you move through each step of the gradual release progression. Many teachers have had lots of success introducing comprehension strategies in a whole-group launch lesson (show) and then doing follow-up instruction (share/support/sustain) at the small-group and individual levels.

The possibilities are endless and vary based on each situation and its students. Allow for options around this element as your learners' responses indicate, and consider whether making shifts in group size can make your scaffolding more effective.

CONSIDER ADJUSTING DEGREES OF SUPPORT

Remember, things are rarely black and white. Some areas need a heavier scaffold, and others may require a lighter touch, and finding the just-right fit in the moment will depend on how tuned in you are to your students and their growth. Besides moving up or down the gradual progression or faster and slower through its stages, other opposing ranges can also help you identify places where you can modify your instruction.

For example, you might offer stronger or weaker support within each stage, depending on how your kids are progressing. Some learners might require more substantial physical, visual, or auditory scaffolds (n.), whereas others would just as easily benefit from a slighter one. As with the other indicators we've discussed in the flexible delivery triangle, where your teaching should fall in the scale of things will be determined by what your students tell you they need throughout their evolution toward the goal.

A familiar option is to adjust the difficulty of the activity you're asking the learner to do. Somewhere in the range between hard and easy, this concept considers whether the activity meets learners where they are, so it can support them as they move toward independence. For instance, say I'm building word ladders with students and want them to take the word *thin* and make it say *chin*. Consider the following scale of activity:

- Change the *first two letters* to make it say *chin*.

- Change *just two letters* to make it say *chin*.

- Change the *beginning sound* to make it say *chin*.

- Change *the word* and make it say *chin*.

Notice that each one requires a slight increase in what the learner needs to control to be successful. We could raise the difficulty further by replacing the word *chin* in each example with a meaningful clue such as "Change the first two letters to make it say a part of your face." Depending on their readiness, we could move up or down these degrees of difficulty as necessary to find the right fit to suit our learners' needs.

CONSIDER CHANGING HOW YOU SAY IT

If you've ever been in a disagreement, you know from experience that what people say and how they say it can make a huge difference in your response. It's the same in the scaffolding progression. If your students aren't gaining independence in the way you'd anticipated, it may be that a slight adjustment in your wording would move your instruction in the right direction. This could be moving to a more child-friendly way of saying something, trying a different way of explaining, or even repeating your directions with pauses in between to check for understanding.

During a fifth-grade reading conference a few years ago, I was reminded how much even small changes in wording matter. Andrew was reading Kathi Appelt's incredible book *The Underneath,* and we were focusing on monitoring the plotline in chapter books. If you've read it, you'll remember that Appelt beautifully weaves separate plotlines throughout the book until they eventually merge into a satisfying ending. But to get to that ending, the reader really has to hang in there and keep the different story lines sorted along the way. To help him work things out, I was using the phrase *multiple plotlines*, but somehow that didn't click with Andrew. What was interesting was how in his retelling, Andrew would use the word *meanwhile* to sort things out for himself: "Meanwhile under the house . . ." and "Meanwhile back at the swamp . . ." In the midst of another attempt to get him to see it my way, it hit me that what Andrew was referring to as *meanwhile* was really his way of articulating multiple plotlines. After that, we started referring to the concept of different story lines in the same text as *meanwhiles*, and now when I'm helping readers with similar confusions, I start out using this notion to lay the groundwork before moving on to the concept of multiple plotlines.

Be open to modifying the way you say things. Listen for what resonates with your learners. Initially naming a period as a stop sign or mental images as pictures in your mind to get your point across may offer just the right level of verbal support to lay foundations you can build on later when you introduce the appropriate academic language.

In this section, we're only scratching the surface with this concept. It goes deeper. Much deeper. So much so, that Chapters 6 and 7 are devoted to what we say, how we say it, and the effects that feedback can have on our scaffolds and our learners' level of independence.

Working with a mind-set of assessment takes time and practice, but the more you do it, the more confident you'll become. And though there may be times when everything stops and you spread your observation notes out in a quiet spot to think, this process more often happens on the run, with you on your feet in the middle of teaching. That means you'll want to stay flexible.

This is no small calling. Scaffolding is multidirectional and multidimensional. It's holistic, diverse, simultaneous, and responsive. Based on your intentional observations and rooted in your thoughtful decisions, your scaffolds will flex and shift into an interwoven pattern of support that evolves steadily as learners take on increasing degrees of independence across the gradual release progression.

CONSTRUCTIVE REFLECTIONS

1. Think about an instructional plan you had to completely abandon. What kept this lesson from being successful? What could you have done differently in the planning stages that might have helped?

2. Are you a kid watcher? What are your observational practices, and how could you refine them?

3. What barriers, if any, do you experience that keep you from being as observant as you'd like? How could you address them in a productive way?

4. How much do you trust your teacher's intuition? In what situations are you more likely (or less likely) to act decisively based on your observations of student behaviors?

5. Recall a lesson you've taught that didn't go quite the way you'd planned. Which point of the flexible delivery triangle seems to have been the issue? Were you unclear about your student needs, were you working from a skewed focus, or did your instruction need some adjusting? What steps might you take to avoid this in the future?

6. Are there any stages of the gradual release progression you tend to neglect or give too much attention to? Why do you think that is? How might adjusting this affect your scaffolds?

PART THREE

FEEDBACK

Strong scaffolds exist and expand in an ongoing feedback loop that emphasizes and builds on students' thinking so they can monitor how they're doing and take the next, right steps toward independence.

CHAPTER 6 THE FEEDBACK LOOP:
OBSERVING, REFLECTING, AND RESPONDING

I teach in a suburb where I'd swear the city's only revenue is the money they collect from giving speeding tickets. At every entrance are signs announcing, "Welcome to Windcrest!" and then just below each one hangs a catchall speed limit sign that simply says, "20 miles per hour unless otherwise noted."

But here's the thing: it's never *otherwise noted*. The entire town is twenty miles per hour! Talk about a speeding ticket waiting to happen. And you can't say you weren't warned. It's the talk of the town. From the moment you move here, everyone from neighbors to coworkers emphatically warns you, "Whatever you do . . . don't speed in Windcrest. You *will* get a ticket."

You'd think that, what with all the posted signs and a near-urban-legend status—not to mention the fact that my school faces the city's police station—I wouldn't speed there.

But I do.

Correction: I did. That is, until the city decided to do something about it. At first, they posted a police officer just down the street from the school. Sure, I'd slow down if I saw him, but if there was no car in sight, I wasn't very mindful of my speed. Eventually, they just started parking an empty police car in the same spot every day. At first, I'd tap my brakes a little, but as soon as I could see there was no one actually in the car to give me a ticket, I went back to my old habits.

Then one day, the city got clever and put in one of those radar speed limit signs. You know—the one that looks like a traditional speed limit sign but, just below it, a radar display announces how fast you're going as you drive by it.

That new sign changed everything. Each time I approached it, I'd tap my brakes, check my speed against the sign, and, if I was going a little too fast, fix it immediately. Before long, I noticed that every time I looked at my speedometer, I was driving a perfect twenty miles per hour. It had all just become habit.

What's interesting is that nothing had really stopped me from watching my speed before. In fact, I had plenty of supports at my disposal: a speedometer in my car, police cars (manned or unmanned) scattered all about town, and insistent reminders from anyone who's ever been caught speeding in Windcrest. Why were things different just because of a little sign?

A *Wired* magazine article shed some light on this for me. The writer discusses similar scenarios, highlighting research about how radar signs like mine are effective because they capitalize on the principles of the *feedback loop*, a concept largely developed through the work of Stanford psychologist Albert Bandura. These loops occur when we're continually given specific data about where we stand in light of a particular objective, inviting us to evaluate our progress and then take action. In other words, assuming we don't want a speeding ticket, a radar sign giving us real-time information about exactly how fast we're going makes it more likely that we'll adjust our driving toward that goal (Goetz 2011).

The article goes on to discuss how modern technologies are taking advantage of feedback loops to change human behaviors for the better. But my thinking detoured to the way this same pattern reinforces our instructional scaffolds when we work with students in the construction zone. In a manner of speaking, the way we question, prompt, cue, interact, and encourage learners can act as figurative radar signs, each reflecting how students are doing—in real time—so they can take immediate action.

But note that these interactions aren't one-time, one-way events. In truth, they operate in rotations over time, where we survey student efforts, offer feedback, observe how they respond, reflect on what we're noticing, and give them more feedback in light of what we see. In this way, our scaffolding language continues to circle back and forth between our students and us—with each cycle moving them closer and closer to success. With this blueprint in mind, we investigate scaffolding's third common condition:

> *Effective scaffolds exist and expand in a responsive feedback loop that continually moves learners toward greater degrees of mastery.*

A feedback loop is defined as "the pathway by which information about the results of a process is sent back to modify or control the process" (Harris and Hodges 1995, 83). That's the technical definition. In reality, this happens all the time. Say you're on a diet (the process). Once a week, you weigh yourself to see how you're doing (information about the results of the process) so you can keep up the good work or adjust your eating habits (modify or control the process). Assuming you still want to lose weight, you'll continue this process week after week (continual feedback loop) until you achieve your final goal weight. Even then, you'll likely choose to continue weekly weigh-ins to maintain your success.

Essentially, this is what our feedback loops do within our scaffolds. When we hold a specific goal in sight while giving learners consistent, constructive information about how they're doing in relation to the goal, we create a clearer, more informed path across the zone of proximal development. And just like a radar sign or regular weigh-ins, our constant feedback invites students to monitor their process as they get closer and closer to the goal. For instance, consider the following writing conference with Lucas, who is working on improving his leads:

Teacher:

Tell me what you're working on.

Lucas:

I'm writing about when my paw-paw went in the hospital.

Teacher:

I remember that. That was a sad time for you.

Lucas:

Yeah.

Teacher:

I think it's really brave that you're writing about it.

Lucas:

Yeah? Maybe . . . but I'm trying to get the first part right.

Teacher:

You want a really strong lead . . .

Lucas:

Yeah . . . but I don't think the one I have is good.

Teacher:

Okay. Tell me what's not working about it.

Lucas:

It just feels boring . . .

Teacher:

Read it out loud for yourself, and let's hear how it sounds.

Lucas:

"When my paw-paw got sick last year, we had to take him to the hospital."

Teacher:

What's not working in it for you?

Lucas:

Like I said, it's boring.

Teacher:

I wonder if what you mean is that it doesn't really tell your readers how serious it all was. I remember you had to rush him downtown.

Lucas:

Yeah. We were all running around and scared. It was the middle of the night.

Teacher:

Oh. Yeah, that does sound scary. Could you just say that?

Lucas:

Just say we were running around scared?

Teacher:

Sure. If you want to. How could you work that in? [*glances at anchor chart*] You know . . . to figure out a new lead.

Lucas:

[*follows teacher's glance*] Oh . . . I could try out three different leads and see which one sounds best.

Teacher:

Yeah. I think that's smart. Think about that night . . . when it all first started . . . what you were feeling and doing . . . and try writing that moment a few different ways.

Lucas:

Okay. I think I know what to do now.

Teacher:

I bet you do. I'll circle back around in few minutes to see how you're doing.

What probably struck you first is the way his teacher's responses show Lucas that she cares for him and his experiences and believes he can do well. This type of encouraging relationship between the more knowing other and the learner is so important to the effectiveness of our instructional feedback loops that we'll return to it in detail when we take a closer look at the qualities of constructive feedback in the next chapter.

But beyond her compassionate demeanor, notice how Lucas's teacher continually gives him feedback and, with each successive response, guides him nearer to independently writing an effective lead. As we scaffold students through learning experiences like this, our immediate feedback emphasizes and builds on their thinking, so they can monitor how they're doing. The way you respond might help students clarify their process, remind them of a forgotten strategy, encourage them to try a more effective approach, or even join them as they celebrate their success. In this way, we raise their awareness by bringing things to their conscious level, so they can see whether what they're doing is working or not working and think about what they could do that might work better.

We see an example of this in a second-grade teacher helping a young writer edit for ending marks. As her teacher reads through a few paragraphs out loud without stopping for a breath or a meaningful pause, the writer immediately sees the problem and remembers the importance of using ending marks appropriately. Together, then, they read through and edit the piece with the teacher continuing to give awareness-building feedback by periodically asking, "Think about where you want your readers to stop along the way. There? Okay. Then what ending mark do you want to put there to tell them that?"

Here are other examples of feedback that encourage students to be reflective:

- Read it again and listen to how you string your words together.

- What's your plan?

- What were you thinking when you read that?

- Were you right?

- Did that work for you?

- Tell me about what you were hoping your readers would visualize when they read this.

- What makes you say that?

- Let me see if I got this right. You're thinking . . . [*sum up student thinking*]

- How did you do that? Share your strategy with us.

As you work to strengthen your scaffolds, be intentional about how your interactions make learners more aware of the strategic actions they're taking, so they can evaluate their progress and take the next step in the right direction.

OBSERVE, REFLECT, AND RESPOND: FUELING THE FEEDBACK LOOP

Every scaffolding experience is unique—each with its own set of players, each with its own dynamics, and each working at varying plot points across the gradual release progression. It makes sense, then, that the work children do in these individualized scaffolding situations would demand thoughtful, tailor-made responses. Effective instructional feedback loops are driven by a sequence of actions on our part that moves from *observing* our learners, to *reflecting* on their needs and personalities, and then *responding* with the most appropriate feedback to guide them closer to independence.

Observe

In earlier chapters, we explored the responsive characteristics of scaffolding and took special care to connect the role assessment plays in that process. Here, we apply those same qualities of assessment to feedback. For the most part, the constructive feedback you give your students throughout the scaffolding process will be driven by the informal, moment-by-moment observations you're making as you work alongside them in the zone of proximal development. Building on the fifth S, survey, listen in and observe your students' behaviors with your focus clearly in mind. Ask questions, gather data, and monitor how they're reacting to your instruction.

Reflect

Using your observations of student behaviors and reactions, think about where they are in their journey to independence and what they will need next. Interpret the information you've collected and make an informed decision about what feedback would support your learners best. At this stage, ask yourself these questions:

- What meaning do I place on all this evidence I'm seeing?

- Based on that evidence, where are we in relation to the goal?

- What is the most effective feedback I could give right now?

- What can I say or do to help this learner move closer to independence?

Respond

Grounded in your observations and reflective decision making, respond with purposeful feedback that helps learners see options. Be sure to express your feedback in a supportive, kid-friendly way that's clear and practical. Above all, remember that the purpose of your feedback is to help students see how they're doing, recalibrate if needed, make a choice, and take action.

In the following example, notice how this practice of observing, reflecting, and responding helps us determine the best feedback to give next. Say we *observe* the readers below, who, at first glance, missed the same word on a recent small-group running record. The original sentence read, "The chickens played in the yard."

Reader One: The [*looks at picture*] animals played in the yard.

Reader Two [*quickly*]: The sun played in the yard.

Reader Three: The ch- [*waits, searches the text and picture, looks up at the teacher for help, and searches again, until finally the teacher tells him the word*—chickens] played in the yard.

Reader Four: The [*waits*] children played in the yard.

How would you respond to each student's attempt with constructive feedback that would make future efforts more successful? Certainly this is the same missed word—but it's not caused by the same misconceptions, and because of this, won't merit the same response. When it comes to effective feedback, there's no room for a one-size-fits-all mentality. What you say must be directly tailored to fit the level of need in each individual situation.

First we need to *reflect* on our observations and what we know about these students. For instance, would it affect your response to know that Reader Three is an ELL student who's still in his first few years of speaking English? Or that Reader Two can tell you her last name, *Charles*, has the *ch* team in it? What if I told you the first reader's teacher has been working with him for several lessons now to use picture meaning for support? Or—and, if I've done my job right—would you like to know considerably more about these children before you decide?

Clearly, how you'd *respond* in a feedback loop depends on the specific child and scaffolding situation you're in. This customized response considers multiple sources of information:

- *Past Instructional Experience:* What type of teaching has this student been exposed to that will prepare him for this feedback?

- *Background Knowledge:* What does the student already bring to the table that this feedback can build on?

- *Readiness:* How prepared is this student for the next level of responsibility in the learning continuum?

- *Approximations:* How close are this student's current attempts to the target, and what feedback will move him closer?

- *Level of Independence:* Where are we in the gradual release progression, and what can I say or do that will move the student further across the zone of proximal development?

Look back at what we observed in the third reader's efforts and think about how these considerations might help his teacher craft a helpful response. Even though she had to tell him the word (*chickens*), seeing his *approximations* at the point of difficulty tells us quite a lot about him as a reader. It's obvious that somewhere along the way, he was taught to use several strategies (*past instructional experiences*). He attempts the first sound, looks at the picture, searches the text, and even returns to searching when his teacher doesn't respond to his first appeal for help. Using everything at his disposal, he takes as much responsibility as possible for attacking this unknown word. However, despite this strong level of *independence* in problem solving, our young reader is still unsuccessful. His teacher, seeing all of this in the moment, seems to have suspected that he didn't know the English word for chickens (*background knowledge*) and felt it best at the time to simply tell him the word and move on. Considering all of this, perhaps the most constructive response she could offer would be to name and affirm all the strategic attempts this young reader made so he'll keep doing them and then take advantage of the moment to directly introduce the word *chickens* so he can begin to incorporate this new word into his English vocabulary (*readiness*).

Like a soccer player constantly adjusting his moves to the second-by-second fluctuations in the game, helpful feedback loops are fueled by an ability to *observe* your students, *reflect* on what you're seeing, *respond* constructively, and then plow forward—all on the run. This is essentially what formative assessment is all about: using data to respond in the moment so students can recalibrate if needed. Granted, this takes quick wit and a keen eye, and at first, it may not come naturally to you. But that's okay. Over time and with practice, observing, reflecting, and responding to children through feedback loops will become an automatic part of your regular teaching practices.

One final note about feedback loops. You may have already noticed that in a typical scaffolding scenario, there are, in fact, two feedback loops in play. One is based on the feedback we give our students about their efforts, and the other is based on the reflection their behaviors mirror at us about the effectiveness of our teaching.

Effective scaffolds exist in a reciprocal feedback loop where the teacher and student each inform the actions of the other. For instance, when we look back at the earlier writing conference between Lucas and his teacher, Lucas was adjusting his process in light of the feedback his teacher was giving him, but even as that was happening, his responses were giving her indicators about what her next instructional steps should be.

This highlights the give-and-take nature of the feedback loop and how, even as we're giving our students feedback, their behaviors are informing us—in real time—about the effects of our instructional language on their progress toward the scaffolding goal. In a constant cycle of interactions like these, the feedback loop drives a continual pattern where our instructional efforts are brought to light, giving us the opportunity to monitor their effects and correct or confirm our attempts.

In the previous chapter, we examined how attending closely to children's efforts can inform our need for flexibility and discussed how, to do this effectively, we stay in a constant mind-set of assessment. This same concept of watchfulness plays a pivotal role in our responses. Feedback is just as much about attentive listening and observing as anything else, and feedback loops are a demonstration of the larger assessment-based, responsive qualities of scaffolding itself. At the same time we're letting students know how they're doing, we're in constant survey mode, monitoring the effects of our own work so we can respond appropriately, with the exact feedback language they need to move closer to independence.

In essence, our students' responses drive our next level of feedback.

CONSTRUCTIVE REFLECTIONS

1. What personal experiences do you have with feedback loops (for example, radar signs, regular weigh-ins, and so on)? How do feedback loops help you monitor yourself while keeping you focused on a goal, and how can those experiences inform the way you give instructional feedback?

2. Reflect on your recent scaffolding interactions. To what degree does your current level of feedback support your students in assuming responsibility for their own learning and making strategic steps toward independence? Could you be more intentional with this?

3. In what ways does your feedback build students' awareness into their own processes? Do your responses help them monitor their thinking? How could you do this better?

4. With so many factors that need your attention in the scaffolding process, how do you tailor your feedback so that it's responsive? Are you satisfied with this or is this an area that could use some fine-tuning?

5. As you move through a lesson, in what ways do you allow your students' responses to guide your own? Are you thinking about what you'll say next, or are you waiting to observe what your children do first? How much energy do you spend in reflection before responding to their efforts?

6. How fluid is your ability to observe, reflect, and respond with appropriate feedback? Is it instinctive at this point in your career, or are you just now learning the process? In what ways could you improve in this area?

CHAPTER 7

CONSTRUCTIVE FEEDBACK:
RESPONDING IN WAYS THAT FOSTER INDEPENDENCE

Young readers and writers place enormous importance on the feedback we give them. Through what we say and how we say it, they readily infer our mood, our authenticity, or even our level of frustration. And, though it might be a wholly unconscious conclusion, children also have no trouble figuring out how we perceive them and their abilities.

Plainly put: our words have power and potential. They can encourage effort, communicate assurance, convey expectation, or express confidence. And, they can just as easily shift thoughts, shape ideas, clarify misunderstandings, and celebrate independence.

In the last chapter we looked at the responsive nature of feedback loops and how these cumulative cycles work together to move learners closer and closer to independence. Picking up there, this chapter is about constructive feedback—the growth-producing things we say within those loops to scaffold readers across the zone of proximal development. Essentially, it's about the dynamic, moment-by-moment conversations we use to teach, inform, question, and observe students in the construction zone.

But constructive feedback also includes being with and relating to students in ways that send messages of support and encouragement. In other words, it isn't just about *what* we say. It's also about *how* we say it.

To the casual observer, these interactions might look like normal, everyday conversation between a teacher and student. But upon closer investigation, you'll see an absolute reason behind each exchange. What you say and how you say it can send ripples through your scaffolds, so you'll want to ensure that, in each moment of the gradual release progression, you're fully aware of the purpose behind the feedback you're giving.

QUALITIES OF CONSTRUCTIVE FEEDBACK

One of the most versatile and powerful techniques in a teacher's toolbox, effective feedback can increase motivation, raise achievement, and contribute to a student's self-extending system long after the scaffold is removed (Rutherford 2012). But what characteristics make our feedback particularly more or less constructive than anything else we might say during the scaffolding process? How can we make the nature of our feedback just as intentional as the rest of our scaffold?

The right feedback placed at just the right time can make the difference between mediocre teaching and powerful instruction, and certain qualities lend themselves to this task better than others. As we look at the qualities of constructive feedback, remember that what we say must be encouraging, useful, thought-provoking, and timely—all while sending students the message that they can take responsibility to effect their own success. But above all, effective feedback is grounded in an encouraging relationship with a caring, more knowing other.

CONSTRUCTIVE FEEDBACK IS GROUNDED IN SUPPORTIVE RELATIONSHIPS

As we talk, think, and work alongside children to co-construct new learning, the positive rapport we establish can stimulate their brain's frontal lobes, releasing endorphins that make learning more enjoyable and effective (Sousa 2011). This probably resonates with you because you've seen it firsthand. Think back to an enjoyable learning experience you've had in the past. Likely, your more knowing other spoke to you in just the right way that supported your learning and made you feel safe.

Our young readers and writers need these same things. In his book *Teaching with Poverty in Mind*, Eric Jensen (2009) argues that because students come to us with a hardwired drive for these types of safe, reliable connections, "The relationships that teachers build with students form the single strongest access to student goals, socialization, motivation, and academic performance" (20). In other words, when we build caring relationships with children and speak to them patiently in ways that send positive messages of support and interest, they'll move mountains to learn with us.

Effective instructional scaffolds—and the feedback loops that guide them—are driven by these types of supportive teacher-student relationships (Vygotsky 1978). When our feedback communicates an emotional level of support, we motivate learners and positively affect classroom behaviors. But to accept that feedback, children need to trust the person giving it. We set the tone. Genuine interactions delivered in a positive tone of voice with caring mannerisms help solidify a message that says, "I'm someone you can talk with. I'm someone who will listen. And this is a safe place for you to grow."

Be cautious about assuming your kids automatically know this. For a long time, I took it for granted, until one day, I actually asked. At the time, Kristen, a third grader, was having an incredibly difficult time getting a particular concept, so I stopped the lesson to investigate. "Kristen, are you okay?" I asked. She looked back at me, obviously frustrated. "Don't worry," I encouraged, "you'll get it." Again, she just stared back at me. She wasn't buying it. Curious, I asked, "Do you believe you can do it?"

"No," she whispered after a few seconds.

Her reply concerned me. How was she ever going to improve if she didn't think it was possible? Even more curious, I asked, "Kristen, do you think *I* believe you can do it?" Her shrug in response was just as disheartening. Even if she had some notion of my faith in her, she obviously wasn't convinced.

From that moment forward, I vowed to make my interactions with all my students supportive and encouraging. I want them to know that I have compassion for what they're going through and believe wholeheartedly that they will be successful.

And I want my feedback to send that message loud and clear.

One of the main ways we let students know we care about them during the scaffolding process is by remaining present and attentive. It can be difficult when we're being pulled in so many different directions, but giving children our undivided attention fosters strong relationships that support our feedback in ways that are immeasurable.

- Use a positive tone of voice and caring mannerisms.

- Take time to visit with students in ways that show genuine interest in who they are, how they got there, and where they're going. Ask about their lives, check in about their struggles, and get to know their goals.

- Give learners time to respond, and listen to those responses.

- Laugh with children and let them see your human side.

- Ask kids for their thoughts and opinions—and take steps to incorporate them.

- Treat all children with respect and allow no less from their peers.

- Listen attentively—if you can't do so immediately, be sure to set aside some time to follow up with them and honor it.

Building strong relationships also requires us to take the time to see the situation through the learner's eyes—to really dig deep to see what they're thinking and how they're feeling. The essential message in this type of empathetic responding is "I care about you, I believe in you, I want to understand your experience, and I work from the unconditional assumption that you are fully capable of success." Consider the following interaction between fourth grader Brianna and her teacher:

Teacher:
Can I help? You look stuck.

Brianna:
Yeah. I'm okay. Just trying to decide on my next book.

Teacher:
Well, what's your pile looking like?

Brianna:
I'm down to these two, and now I just have to pick.

Teacher:
Okay . . . so . . . tell me what you're thinking.

Brianna:

Well, I've never read anything like this one, so I might try it, but . . .
remember that book about the bear we read last week in group?

Teacher:

Sure . . . I remember you really liked that one.

Brianna:

Well . . . yeah . . . I did . . . and this one is by that same lady . . . but it's about wolves.

Teacher:

I see. Does that help you make your decision?

Brianna:

I think so. I mean . . . I liked her other book. *[thinks a moment]* I think I'm gonna try this one.

Teacher:

Sounds like a plan to me.

Notice how, in this brief interaction, her teacher gives feedback in ways that let Brianna know she

- cares about her (Can I help? You look stuck);

- wants to understand her experience (Tell me what you're thinking);

- believes in her abilities as a learner (Sounds like a plan to me); and

- is tuned in to her processes as a learner (I remember you really liked that one. Does that help you make your decision?).

All of these responses encourage Brianna to continue her thinking, trust her intuition, and strive for a greater degree of independence. As you work with your own students, think about how your feedback can support them in similar ways. Further examples of empathetic feedback might include responses such as these:

- I notice that you . . .

- Tell me more . . .

- Help me understand . . .

- How did you feel about that?

- Talk to me about . . .

- When you did [the attempt], what were you telling yourself?

- Share with me how you worked that out.

- It looks like you were thinking [assumption]. Am I right?

- Share your thinking . . .

- I can see this is important to you.

- What makes you say that?

- Can you show me the hard part? What was difficult about it?

- I can tell you're excited/frustrated/not sure . . .

- I wonder if you . . .

As you refine your relationships with students, you'll also want to be intentional about your nonverbal discourse and how it supports your words in sending messages of confidence, empathy, and empowerment. The best response in the world delivered with indifferent body language, tone, and expression will likely fall flat, so another way you can support students is to stay mindful of the unspoken communications you may be less aware of. It's not enough for learners to hear our words of encouragement; they also need to be able to see and sense our intent. The nonverbal ways in which you listen and respond radiate your genuineness and reinforce your verbal feedback.

Most of us would be surprised at just how many of our interactions with children are nonverbal—not to mention the lasting effects they can have. I once watched a teacher confer with a second-grade student after she listened to him read. She brought him back to a page he'd trudged through and pointed out a difficult part he'd been able to figure out on his own. "Wow! I noticed how you had some trouble with this word right here. You stopped, got real quiet, and looked up at me. Then you looked over at the picture, waited a few more seconds, and you got it."

"Yeah," he said, a smile of pride spreading across his face. "It was really hard!"

"I saw that. It took a lot of work!" his teacher responded. "Can you tell me what you were thinking when you stopped and got so quiet? How'd you figure it out?"

"Well," he said pensively, "at first I thought I couldn't do it . . . and then I looked at you . . . and I could tell you thought I could . . . so . . . I just did it!"

Even though that probably wasn't what this teacher was going for, her young reader was trying to articulate something just as important. But you might not have noticed it if you hadn't been watching for it. When this reader stopped and glanced at his teacher for help on that hard word, she simply winked and smiled and looked back at him with an encouraging expression that seemed to say, "I have faith in you. You can do this."

Interactions like this, in which we send powerful messages without speaking a word, illustrate how our nonverbal communication can support our spoken feedback to convey caring and build relationships with students. Below are a few additional pointers to consider:

- Work with students at their level—pull up a chair, sit on the floor, or kneel beside them.

- Nod to show you're listening.

- Adjust your facial expressions to show interest, concern, or contemplation.

- Smile. Really. Sometimes it's easy to forget.

- Make and maintain caring eye contact with them.

- Use a tone that conveys interest when you speak.

- Give learners your undivided attention and listen attentively, completely focused and engaged in what they're saying.

- Keep an open stance and relaxed posture, leaning forward to show interest.

Coaching children to continuously reach just beyond what they can already do requires a great deal of expertise on our part. But it also involves compassion, understanding, kindness, and thoughtfulness. The zone of proximal development can be an intimidating place filled with new challenges at every turn, tentative levels of knowledge, and an understandable measure of cautious self-doubt. In addition to helping learners navigate their next academic steps, one of the roles you play, as a more knowing other, is that of an encourager—standing side by side with students, sending messages of support and reassurance.

If we want kids to value the feedback we provide and take risks in their learning, it is imperative that we establish and maintain strong, supportive relationships in which they're engaged, motivated, and ready to participate in the learning process with us. This is further evidence of what we already know to be true: when we show our students that we care about them and their learning, and take time to communicate it, they're inspired to work harder with us.

When we're intentional about these relationships, the hidden messages behind our words assure children with conviction and certainty, "You're not alone. I believe in you, and I'll be right here with you until you're ready do it without me."

CONSTRUCTIVE FEEDBACK IS PROCESS DRIVEN

For years, we've been taught the importance of praise. Responding to students with language such as "Good job!" or "I like the way you figured that out" has long been endorsed by conventional wisdom as a way to improve student engagement, motivation, and growth. But feedback that focuses on students' personality traits or abilities can also have adverse effects that we aren't even aware of (Pink 2009; Kamins and Dweck 1999). For instance, if I say, "Good job, Megan," I run the risk of Megan's motivation becoming dependent on my approval of her work. And even though "I like the way you figured that out, Megan" nods to a strategic attempt on her part, opening with "I like . . ." could just as easily send a message that her work is all about pleasing me.

In his book *Opening Minds: Using Language to Change Lives*, Peter Johnston (2012), building on the work of Carol Dweck (2006), connects these dots for us by differentiating between students who work from a *fixed-performance* outlook, seeing their plight as prearranged and unchangeable, and those who work from a *dynamic-learning* perspective, from which they see possibilities and feel empowered to pursue them. Johnston further distinguishes between feedback that is *process oriented* (based on work, strategy, and effort) and *person oriented* (driven by personality, judgment, and teacher-pleasing qualities) and explains how the form we use can contribute to lasting effects

	PERSON-ORIENTED FEEDBACK (UNHELPFUL)	PROCESS-ORIENTED FEEDBACK (CONSTRUCTIVE)
Examples	"I'm proud of you." "How impressive . . . You're one smart cookie." "You're doing a good job!" "You're a good reader."	"You gave it some thought and figured out a different way to do it!" "You looked at the picture and made it make sense." "The way you added factual details helps your readers understand how sharks hunt for food." "When you grouped your words together while you read, it sounded just like talking."
Implied Message	Traits like being a good reader and being smart are inherent—you either are or you're not. Your level of success is dependent on whether your work pleases or disappoints me.	Success comes from hard work and strategic thinking You are capable of evaluating your work, gauging your success, and deciding if you're pleased with your efforts, and you're free to do so.
Outlook Influenced	Fixed-Performance	Dynamic-Learning
Possible Effects	• Believe that we are born with abilities and there's not much we can do to change them • See difficulty as defeating • May not believe strategy or effort matters • Self-blame and helplessness • Attribute future achievement to innate ability	• Believe talent can be grown through perseverance and effort • See difficulty as a challenge • Believe effort can affect growth • Self-reliance • Attribute future achievement to determined effort

Figure 7.1
Person-Oriented Feedback Versus Process-Oriented Feedback

on whether learners believe they can change or improve their outcomes. Essentially, person-oriented feedback encourages a fixed-performance frame of mind, and process-oriented feedback contributes to a dynamic-learning perspective (see Figure 7.1).

The good news, Johnston argues, is that we can capitalize on this principle to craft feedback that inspires students' confidence in their capacity to effect their own success. Consider, for instance, "You thought about what you already knew that could help you" or "When you wrote about the beach house, the words you used helped me visualize it clearly." In these examples, the feedback calls attention to the student's process—the steps she took and the productive results of her actions, strategy, and effort—rather than evaluating the worth or teacher-pleasing qualities of her attempts.

Remember, the purpose of constructive feedback is to help learners change and grow. If we want them to take steps to improve, then what we say to them has to empower a belief structure that change and growth are, in fact, possible. In view of this, constructive feedback is process driven. It isn't about blessing or blame. It isn't about approval or disapproval. Instead it focuses on the behaviors, rather than the person, responding objectively—without judgment or hidden messages of personal worth or value—to help students monitor their work, so they can clearly see what was successful and what needs some revision.

CONSTRUCTIVE FEEDBACK IS USEFUL

The process-oriented examples of feedback in Figure 7.1 all have one thing in common. They all offer students something they can capitalize on and actually use. For instance, "How impressive . . . You're one smart cookie" may feel nice to hear, but it isn't constructive. Nothing in that statement gives learners something to take away and apply in future situations. On the other hand, feedback like, "You gave it some thought and figured out a different way to do it!" implies that what they did was effective and that if they're stuck later, they could do it again. Think about the internalized message that helps establish "I'm a person who looks for alternative solutions when things get rough." This is definitely an empowering strategy children could apply in the future.

This highlights a critical characteristic of constructive feedback: it has to be useful. What we say should accentuate something learners can apply immediately or draw on for support later. Process-oriented feedback fits this bill, because it expects, looks for, and promotes strategic thinking, making room for the possibility that learners can take action to effect their success.

Above all else, useful feedback is action oriented—effectively asking, "How can what I'm saying right now, in this moment, support my students where they are and move their thinking forward so they can take that next, strategic step toward the ultimate goal of independence?"

- Do they need some information to help them move ahead?

- Should they continue something that's working?

- Do they need a quick reminder?

- Would it help for them to look at things in a new way?

- Could they try a different approach?

The goal here is for students to take an active part in their own learning. Effective scaffolders work hard to ensure that the feedback they give students urges them toward a decisive response. Whether we're summarizing their progress, helping them see where things broke down, or highlighting behaviors that played a part in their success, our interactions with students need to make them think about their process and call them to take some sort of action.

But if children are actually going to take such action, it's critical that they clearly understand what we're saying and how capitalizing on our feedback will help them improve. In *How the Brain Learns*, David Sousa (2011) highlights two significant questions that determine the value children place on our instruction: "Does this make sense?" And, "Does this have meaning?" Even though Sousa is primarily discussing the human brain and what it chooses to remember, these criteria can be just as effective in helping us determine whether children find our feedback useful. Literacy teachers Linda Dorn and Tammy Jones (2012) would support this notion. In their book *Apprenticeship in Literacy*, they apply similar standards to our instructional language, pointing out that in addition to ensuring that children clearly understand what we're asking them to do, we must ask ourselves if our responses are meaningful to them and relevant to the goals they're trying to accomplish.

For example, late one fall, Kara moved to our campus and joined one of my reading groups that had been working together since September. Earlier in the season (after a totally unrelated activity making pasta necklaces) the group happened upon a shared way to group words together for fluent phrasing: "thread it up!" By the time Kara showed up, "thread it up" was a regular part of our small-group conversations. A few lessons after she arrived, Kara and I were reading one-on-one when, seeing the need for some fluency practice, I reminded her, "When you read it, remember to thread it up."

I realized my mistake as she scrunched her face up at me, saying matter-of-factly, "I don't even know what that is." Of course she was confused! The words *thread it up* made absolutely no sense to her. Because she hadn't been there for the group's defining pasta necklace moment and its subsequent connection to fluency, my response had no meaning for her either. Despite my best intentions, the feedback I gave her was all but worthless.

How often do we fall into this instructional trap? How often do we respond to young readers and writers with feedback that makes little or no sense and doesn't carry the significance for them we assume it does? If the feedback we're giving children doesn't make sense or have meaning, they quite simply can't use it.

Does your feedback make sense?

To this end, monitor your feedback to make sure you're responding in kid-friendly language that your learners can identify with. Practice being clear and explicit. Be aware of habitual things you say like "thread it together" that may not be obvious to your students or that you haven't actually explained clearly. Recall what you know about flexible and customized responding and recognize, as well, that what makes perfect sense to one student may be a complete mystery to another. For your feedback to be useful, it must be clear enough for your learners to understand where you're going and what you want them to do.

To help keep your responses clear, be careful not to flood kids with feedback. Contrary to what you may have heard, the human brain isn't really wired to multitask, and children have difficulty giving their attention to more than one thing at a time (Medina 2008; Sousa 2011). Giving them too much to take in at one time can confuse children and keep our responses from making sense. Often, especially when kids are having difficulties, it's hard for us to see beyond the surge of teachable moments, and we want to address it all! But even though everything may seem important, overwhelming children with feedback reduces the likelihood that they'll be able to take advantage of it.

For our feedback to be useful, it has to be manageable. Consider responding to one issue at a time and limiting how much feedback you give in one scaffolding session. Think about the most essential area you want to address and consider what you might say in relation to it that will be the most effective. This will definitely take some prioritizing on your part, but it will also increase the possibility that your readers and writers are able to understand what you're saying and act on it.

Does your feedback have relevance to the learner?

It's not enough for children to understand your feedback. For it to be useful, what you say has to be relevant to them and their needs. To this end, you'll want to respond with feedback that is directly applicable to the work they're doing, emphasizing how it will help them so they can put it to work quickly and get results.

Recognize that relevance is different for different people, and just like whether something makes sense or not, what's meaningful to one student may not be to another. To monitor for this, stay in a mind-set of assessment, keeping an eye out for feedback that will be most beneficial by asking yourself these questions:

- Is my feedback something this learner needs to know to move forward?

- Does my response direct this learner to something he can apply right away?

- Will what I'm saying help this learner be successful in other situations beyond this one?

In each instance be sure to connect the relevance of what you're saying by finding ways to emphasize why students need the information you're giving them, how it will help them, and when they would use it.

Another way to keep your feedback meaningful is to help children find ways to articulate their needs in anticipation of your support. For instance, showing young readers and writers how to prepare for conferences so that when you pull up a chair, they're ready to name the specific type of support they need can help concentrate your feedback and make it more relevant. When students see direct connections between your responses and their work, you increase the chances that they'll internalize them and act on them when needed.

Keep in mind that expressing their instructional needs isn't something that comes naturally to many of our kids. This is especially true for students who struggle, and it may not be something that your youngest readers and writers can do just yet. You may need to spend some time coaching them on how to effectively identify what would help them most. Language that can steer your interactions with children through this process might include the following:

- What's not working for you?

- Can you read it again and show me the hard part?

- What kind of help do you need from me?

- Tell me about this paragraph in your writing. What are you trying to do?

- Help me understand what's tricky about it.

- What would you like me to listen for as you read your writing to me?

- Walk me through it up to the part where you got stuck.

Finally, useful feedback isn't afraid to be corrective when necessary. For some people, the idea of teaching as corrective conjures up images of a crotchety schoolmarm who snaps at children with mean-spirited criticism and zero tolerance for error—but that's not what we're talking about here. What we mean when we say "corrective feedback" involves responding to children with clear, descriptive information about what they're doing that's working and what they're doing that's not.

I once had a very spirited exchange with a kindergarten student who was convinced he was making the letter *J* correctly. "Jonathan," I said during a lesson, "since you'll be using the letter *J* a lot, let me show you how to make it."

"Oh, I know how to make it, Mr. Thompson," he said. "It's in my name. See?" He reached over to the whiteboard and wrote his name—with the *J* backward. "There!"

"That's the thing, Jonathan: that's not quite right," I replied, demonstrating. "You're starting off the right way . . . down . . . but when we get to the bottom, we hook it . . . this way."

"No," he said confidently. "It goes the other way."

"You think so? Hmm . . . Let's look at some other *J*s and see if we can find out for sure." I reached for a book nearby, and together, we thumbed through it. "There's one," I said. We studied it and compared it with Jonathan's *J*. "Here's another one. And another one." We continued our investigation, both eager to be proven right.

With each successive example, Jonathan's face tightened a bit more until, finally convinced, he protested, "Aw, man! You mean I've been doing it wrong all this time? How come nobody ever told me?"

Maybe someone had told him and it just hadn't registered at the time. Or perhaps his parents and teachers had other, more pressing, instructional concerns and didn't see forming the letter *J* as a priority for Jonathan just yet. But it's also likely that in being careful not to bruise his spirit, no one thought to simply tell him he was wrong. That's understandable. We want to be considerate with our responses, and I'm not suggesting we berate kids repeatedly. But as Marie Clay (2005) writes, "Children should not be allowed to repeatedly produce miscues in reading and writing on the same words day after day, week after week, because they are consolidating records in their brains that are very difficult to erase" (167). In other words, there will be instances when things simply need to be corrected, and leaving children to sort it out or trusting they'll realize it eventually through guided encounters may not be as helpful as we'd like.

We can be direct without being negative. We can be compassionate while telling students how they could be more effective. Corrective feedback, like the other characteristics we've covered so far, is best when it's encouraging, timely, process driven, and above all, useful. Although it may feel uncaring, it doesn't have to be. Kids deserve to know when a strategy they're using isn't successful or that a misconception is off the mark. And, letting them know with a gentle, considerate hand can be just as useful as any other type of response you could offer.

CONSTRUCTIVE FEEDBACK STIMULATES THINKING

Our scaffolds should give students an opportunity to generate and explore new ideas, to change, and to grow. For children to truly reach independence, our interactions with them have to shift away from customary teacher-as-expert conversations with us simply telling students the answers. Instead, as literacy scholar Regie Routman (2008) stresses, we can help learners best by practicing "responsive teaching" where we "explore students' thinking, help them understand and explain their thinking, and nudge them to a higher level of understanding" (73).

In other words, we want our talk with children to engage their minds and rouse them to contemplate, question, and deliberate. We want them to be thoughtful. But where's the thinking in some of the common types of feedback listed here?

- Yes. That's correct.

- Okay.

- You know that word.

- You got it!

- Try again.

- [*after waiting a few seconds*] Can someone help her out with this question?

Think about my reaction to the radar sign that I described in Chapter 6. My speedometer, the police car, a traffic fine, and even the public shame of being pulled over in the school parking lot didn't really move me to monitor my speed or change my behaviors. Because these factors were on the sidelines, it was easy for me to disregard them. However, when the radar display reflected my speed at me, it engaged my brain, making me more consciously aware of my actions. It made me think more critically about what I was doing—and it was in that thinking that I chose actionable steps that moved me closer to new habits.

Still, how much of our instructional talk, like the bulleted list above, is only peripherally engaging? When we move our feedback to a more constructive stance, we amplify student thinking. Consider this feedback instead:

- Were you right?

- You're on the right track . . . Keep working on it.

- Where could you find the answer?

- How could you be sure?

- You said . . . Does that [sound right, make sense, look right]?

- On a scale of one to ten, how strong is your inference/mental image/ question/summary?

- Talk to your group and see if you're all on the same page.

- Is there something else you could try?

- Who has another way to figure it out that could work just as well?

Effective scaffolders intentionally craft their feedback so it pulls learners in, inspiring them to think and want to learn more. To the highest degree possible, your interactions should engage students' minds and invite thoughtful reflection.

Another way our feedback can do this is by acting as a model and stimulus for the thinking our students will do later on their own. In her book *Reading with Meaning*, Debbie Miller (2013) reminds us that "what you say and how you say it very quickly becomes what they say and how they say it" (73). The act of talking through a process with a more knowing other ultimately encourages learners to internalize new ways of thinking, acting, and speaking that they will eventually carry out on their own. To this end, our feedback can lay the groundwork for "in the head" language that children can take on and ultimately use independently (Vygotsky 1978; Berk and Winsler 1995).

After he had failed three attempts in as many years, I worked with Oscar to help him prepare for his final opportunity to pass the state reading test before middle school. Though he struggled with fluency at times, Oscar's accuracy and comprehension were well up to the task, and he readily identified himself as someone who enjoyed reading. But formal assessments were difficult for him, so we spent several tutoring sessions working on taking the time he needed to read well and how to apply what he already knew to testing situations.

When the results came in, I found Oscar in the hallway to celebrate his passing score with him. I asked him what he had done differently this time around. "I tried hard and I didn't give up," he said. "And the whole test, I remembered all the stuff we talked about, and I kept hearing your voice in my head going, 'You've got this . . . Take your time and make sure you understand it . . . What genre is this and what will you pay attention to as you read it?' It was like you were right there with me." I smiled. To Oscar, it was my voice he heard, but I knew better. In his own way, Oscar was trying to describe how he was beginning to internalize the feedback language I'd been giving him and had returned to it when he needed it on testing day.

Angel-on-the-shoulder incidents like this illustrate how the regular, ongoing feedback we give children can shape their independent self-talk and quickly become part of their thinking process. Thinking together eventually helps us think alone, and one major result of our feedback is that it quickly becomes part of the internalized conversations students have with themselves as self-regulated learners. Eventually, self-talk turns into thought. Constructive feedback takes this into account.

CONSTRUCTIVE FEEDBACK IS TIMELY

Responding at just the right moment, right when kids need it most, is another way we customize our constructive feedback. When author and writing specialist Jeff Anderson visited our campus, we looked on as he led several writing conferences with our students. In one conference, Jeff noticed that although a second grader was incorporating dialogue into her personal narrative, the lack of quotation marks was making it difficult for her (and her audience) to read it. "I see you're telling us what everyone said," he began, "and I bet that will make your readers understand things a lot better." She smiled, and after a few more exchanges about the effectiveness of her dialogue, Jeff said, "Knowing how to show your readers who's talking, though, can get tricky. You know what?" And here, Jeff looked around as if to make sure no one else was listening. "I think you're ready for a writer's secret. Would you like to hear it?" She nodded enthusiastically, and with her full attention, he went on to reveal how using quotation marks could improve her efforts.

In this demonstration, Jeff recognized what this young writer needed most in that moment and capitalized on it by delivering the exact feedback she needed. Because of his timing, she was primed to receive it.

Giving constructive feedback means keeping a thoughtful lookout for well-timed instances when learners are ready to incorporate relevant feedback and responding at the moment when it will be the most effective. Keeping in mind the situational and responsive nature of feedback, here are some other time considerations to think about as you work to improve the effectiveness of your responses:

- *Give learners immediate feedback.* As much as possible, give students real-time information about their efforts, so they can take quick, decisive action toward success. The longer you wait between the student's attempt and your response, the less influence your feedback will have (Johnston 2012; Marzano, Pickering, and Pollock 2001).

- *Give learners time to digest your feedback.* Our feedback can be meaningless if it never has a chance to sink in. Most teachers have a wait time of around three seconds or less, but children learning new material often need more than that. Allowing at least five seconds or more can have positive effects on (1) the length and quality of student responses, (2) the level of participation by needier learners, (3) the amount of evidence students use to support their inferences, and (4) the quantity of higher-order responses students share (Sousa 2011).

- *Give learners time to respond to your feedback.* Once we offer students constructive feedback and time to absorb it, we have to give them a chance to act on it in some way. Although this can be challenging when we feel rushed to cover curriculum or keep up with scheduling demands, children need opportunities to respond to our feedback as we continue to survey their efforts and provide ongoing support.

- *Give learners feedback throughout the scaffolding process.* Feedback should occur in continuous loops across the entire gradual release progression. This would seem to go without saying, but stay aware of it. Sometimes, as learners become more and more independent, we erroneously see their success as evidence that they don't need to hear from us as much, and reduce our amount of feedback. Be cautious if you notice this about yourself. Certainly, the nature of your feedback will change across the gradual release progression (see Chapter 8), but even as children approach independence, they benefit from our feedback cheering them on as they cross the finish line.

Feedback loops find their effectiveness in the timeliness of the information they give. Knowing where learners are along the learning progression and managing the pacing of your responses will help you keep your feedback intentional and effective. In the same way a radar sign reflects real-time information so we can monitor our driving habits, giving learners well-timed feedback throughout the scaffolding process helps them reflect on their attempts, maintaining and self-correcting their behaviors as needed.

EXAMPLES OF CONSTRUCTIVE FEEDBACK

For some teachers, crafting effective feedback comes naturally. Others struggle to find the most powerful thing to say at just the right time. It all takes practice, and responding to learners effectively is a skill that develops over time. As you learn more about feedback, you'll figure out that there are multiple ways to get your point across and that all of them have differing levels of effect on different students. Being familiar with plenty of feedback options, choosing from them instantaneously, and knowing your learners' needs to the highest degree possible will help you differentiate your instruction and responses while keeping your lessons focused. Before long, you'll find yourself on constant lookout, collecting multiple ways to say various things with different degrees of support so you can call on them without hesitation when the time is right.

To support you in this, we'll round out this chapter with several examples of oral language to get you started. Some will sound familiar, others may seem new, and several might help you see additional options beyond the feedback stems you traditionally rely on. Remember, your instructional responses will be as varied as the children you're working with, so of course these lists aren't exhaustive. What's more, the same instructional response can be appropriate in a variety of situations and for multiple reasons, often combining with or complementing other feedback you might give. With that in mind, the framework below represents just one of many ways to look at our instructional language.

As you read on, recall that this book highlights scaffolding from the perspective of the more knowing other. Although that slant is noticeable in the examples, you'll want to note that, practically speaking, our responses actually serve a dual purpose. If our true intention is for what we say and how we say it to become what our children say and how they say it, we have to bear this in mind as we deliver our feedback. Even though our focus here is on how we constructively question, prompt, name, and affirm effective learning behaviors, our ultimate objective is for students to begin to take on these responsibilities as well. For example, at some point, we should stop being the first to recognize a problem requiring a prompt for correction; in the same breath, we don't always want to be the only one celebrating when something goes well. Children can eventually do these things for themselves when we choose our scaffolding language carefully and create experiences from which they learn—from our example—how to initiate inner conversations that guide their progress.

Finally, recognize that these examples aren't intended for memorization, nor would it be realistic for you to thumb through them while teaching in an effort to find just the right response. Instead, I encourage you to use these ideas as springboards to help you organize your thinking, grow your understanding, and practice crafting constructive feedback.

FEEDBACK THAT QUESTIONS

Though feedback is often delivered in the form of a well-placed guiding statement, it's important to note that responding with focused questions can be just as empowering. To be clear, we aren't talking about grilling students in an effort to evaluate them or test their knowledge. Instead, constructive questions are generative, asking in a way that guides learners to

- think about a problem differently *(What else could it be?)*;

- clarify thinking or misunderstandings *(Did that work for you?)*;

- call up a previously controlled strategy *(What have you done before that might help?)*;

- elaborate responses *(What are you thinking?)*; and

- raise their awareness of the effects of their efforts *(What do you notice?)*.

Questioning also helps us gauge where children are so we can alter our feedback to connect with what they already know or spur them to reach just a little bit further in their thinking.

This is a good time to revisit the power of open-ended questions. Simply knowing the difference between open and closed questions and how you use them can make a drastic difference in the way learners respond to your feedback. Closed questions can be answered successfully with a word or two (usually *yes* or *no),* whereas open-ended questions constructively invite expanded answers that generate thoughtful responses. Used too often, closed questions shut our scaffolds down, sending a message that the teacher has all the right answers. In contrast, open-ended questions invite the student in as an active participant in the learning process. And, since open-ended questions leave a wide berth between the right and wrong answer, students can feel safer in taking a risk and sharing their thinking.

I introduce feedback that questions early in this list, because questioning correlates with all the other types of constructive feedback that follow. For instance, you can use questions to prompt learners to try something ("What could you try?"), remind them of a forgotten strategy ("What do you do when you get to a hard word?"), or even affirm their successful efforts ("How did you work that out?"). As you read through the rest of the sections in this chapter, notice the effect of the different feedback questions in contrast to their declarative counterparts in each list of examples. As you do, think about scaffolding situations in which a well-placed question might be just as, if not more, productive.

Examples of language that questions:

- What were you telling yourself when you worked that out?

- Could it be that . . . ?

- What is it you want to do?

- What does this story remind you of?

- Is there another way to look at it?

- What do you already know about it that could help?

- How did you figure that out?

- What from the text makes you say that?

- Does that go with what you know about the story?

- What were you thinking when you . . . ?

- Where are you stuck and how can I help?

- How's it going?

- What did you do to help yourself?

- Where could you look for help?

- You don't seem sure about it . . . What's holding you up?

- What do you remember about . . . ?

- What do you know for sure and what are you not so sure about?

- How does that help you?

- It could be . . . but what if . . . ?

- What do you already know about this topic?

- What worked for you? What didn't?

FEEDBACK THAT DEMONSTRATES

As children reach for new levels of independence, there will be times when the most constructive response you can give is to tell or show students specifically what they'll need to do to be successful. For the most part, this happens at the onset of our scaffolds when we're teaching children something new, but it might also be necessary anywhere along the gradual release sequence when you notice a misconception or confusion that needs to be straightened out— sending you back to the showing part of the 5S progression to reteach and get things back on track.

As we model and demonstrate strategic behaviors for children, we often support these conversations with additional visual or physical scaffolds. In these instances, our verbal feedback should be specific and goal focused, giving students a play-by-play narrative and helping them understand what they need to do to move toward independence.

For example, if I'm working with a kindergartner struggling to match her voice to print, I'd likely start out by explicitly showing her how to point to the words as she reads, inviting her to place her index finger on top of mine as I read, saying, "When I read, I touch each word to make sure what I'm saying matches the words on the page."

Since the more knowing other takes on the bulk of responsibility with this type of feedback, our responses will be far more direct than some of the other examples you'll encounter throughout this chapter. However, note that as students begin to reach higher levels of competence, our feedback should shift in nature (which we'll explore more in the next chapter). So, as my kindergartner progresses from tentative approximations to mastery, my feedback will shift, perhaps moving to "Remember to make it match," and then later pulling back to "Did that match?" and finally moving to "Way to go! You used your finger to make it match!"

With this in mind, be cautious about being unnecessarily explicit, recognizing that the side effects might be less beneficial than we think. In his well-received book *Choice Words*, Peter Johnston (2004) stresses that more accomplished teachers often spend less time being overly explicit and reminds us that "There are hidden costs in telling people things. If a student can figure something out for him- or herself, explicitly providing the information preempts the student's opportunity to build a sense of agency and independence, which, in turn, affects the relationship between teacher and student" (8). Again, this ties in to being reflective and intentional. Knowing your students well and staying aware of their needs will help you make effective choices about how much support they'll need. According to Johnston, "As teachers, we have to decide *what* to be explicit about for *which* students, and *when* to be explicit about it" (8).

Examples of language that demonstrates:

- When you want to [goal], you can [strategic action].

- Watch me do it.

- Do it with me, so you can see what I mean.

- Watch how I say it slowly so I can hear the sounds . . . /f/ . . . /u/ . . . /n/.

- Let me show you how to . . .

- Say it this way . . .

- Watch how I write notes in the margin to help me remember what seems important to me.

- We could say . . . [*Model inference.*]

- Would you like my thinking on that?

- Do this. [*Demonstrate.*]

- I'm going to double the consonant, because . . .

- Write it like this.

- Let's try it again together, but this time . . .

- A lot of writers try [strategic action] like this. [*Demonstrate.*]

- Let me show you how to group your ideas into paragraphs.

- When I see three consonants next to one another, I try to see if they all make a sound together. Let's look. /Str/ . . . string . . .

- I'm going to think about the order of my story before I map it out.

- This is how you show someone is yelling.

- When I read this poem, it makes me think about . . .

- That's not quite it . . . Let me help you out.

- Watch how I break this word into parts I already know that will help me.

- Listen to how I group these words together to make it sound like talking.

- When you're stuck, you can think about what would make sense. I'm thinking . . .

- Look at how I'm [strategy]. This helps me . . .

- Notice how I leave a space there to separate my words when I write.

- When I read this paragraph, I'm making a picture in my mind. I'm imagining . . .

- You can help yourself by [strategic action] . . . like this. [*Demonstrate.*]

FEEDBACK THAT PROMPTS

When we use our feedback to prompt students, we encourage them to do something they've previously been taught to do. Building on and enhancing feedback that demonstrates, which is noticeably explicit, this type of response can be more or less specific, depending on its learner's needs, ranging from a direct call to action to more general hints, cues, and reminders. Think about the differences between the prompt "Look at the picture and think about a word that would make sense there" and its less detailed counterpart "Did it make sense?" Note how the first prompt provides a higher degree of support, whereas the second pulls back, allowing the reader to act with considerably more independence.

Remember, before a prompt can be useful or meaningful, it has to signal problem solving that learners have actually been taught to do, and it has to be within their current level of capability. For instance, prompting a third-grade writer to revise for a strong lead sentence to pull his readers in will likely fall flat if you haven't taken the time to explicitly show him what you mean by "strong lead sentence" or, for that matter, how to craft one.

Whether encouraging emerging behaviors or reminding learners of previously forgotten strategies, effective prompts include statements or questions that nudge young readers and writers to take deliberate strides toward what they almost control.

Examples of language that prompts:

- What could you do to help yourself?

- What could you try?

- Think about how including action here might help show your readers what's happening instead of telling them about it.

- Remember when we talked about . . .

- Does that [make sense/look right/sound right]?

- What else might work?

- When you read that to me, you paused right here [*pointing*] . . . How could you show your readers that you want them to take a breath there?

- Think about what you already know.

- Do you have a picture to help you with that letter sound?

- It could be [approximation] . . . but look at [redirection].

- Tell me more . . .

- Where could you look for help?

- You try it.

- Read that again and [call to action].

- You did some hard work on that tricky word . . . Now try it in the sentence and see if it works.

- What's important to remember when you're reading [a poem/a biography/nonfiction/fiction]?

- Think about your central idea. How could your closing sentence tie back to that?

- How could you use line breaks to make your poem stronger?

- You wrote, "She runned to the playground." Would we say it that way?

- Look at our [anchor chart/prompting card/table tent] and see if that helps.

- When you read it, you said . . . but that doesn't make sense. Try it again and think about the story.

- Read that paragraph out loud and listen for any rough spots in your writing.

- Were you right? How do you know? What else could you check?

FEEDBACK THAT NAMES

Another way our feedback can build on students' strengths is by helping them name what they're already doing well. Here, we ask questions or make statements that encourage students to reflect on and articulate their successful thinking. Pointing out what they've done effectively can support learners at any stage, but it's especially useful when their behaviors are tentative or their attempts are partially correct. This is often when children lack confidence in their new learning, and our constructive feedback can offer assurances by pinpointing what they're doing that's working. Consider this discussion with Mason, who had been learning to work through hard parts on his own without immediately asking me for help:

Mason:

Mom . . . likes him the . . . b-d-e-t . . . likes him the d-b-e-t . . . [waits a few seconds] . . . b-e-st! . . . Mom likes him the best!

Me:

Wow! Look at you! You really worked hard on that and didn't give up. Tell me about it.

Mason:

Well, it was hard the first time and I couldn't get it, but then when I went back, I knew it!

Me:

So, at first you didn't know and then you tried again, and on your second try, you were able to help yourself?

Mason:

Yeah!

Me:

How did you help yourself?

Mason:

I fixed the *b* and made it make sense!

Notice in this exchange how my feedback names what Mason did well ("You worked hard on that and didn't give up" and "At first you didn't know and then you tried again") while encouraging him to articulate more specifically for himself what he did that was so useful ("Tell me about it" and "How did you help yourself?"). Helping Mason name his problem-solving behaviors and identify their positive effects increases the likelihood that they'll become consistent while reinforcing his confidence.

When our feedback calls attention to the best in what young readers and writers are doing, they're more likely to remember successful behaviors and call on them again when they need them. Whether we're highlighting their strengths or encouraging them to do so for themselves, helping learners articulate strategic steps they've taken can help them see their effectiveness and internalize them at a deeper level.

Examples of language that names:

- How did you help yourself?

- What did you try that finally worked? What did you try that didn't?

- You figured it out! If I were stuck like you just were, what would you say that could help me?

- When you got stuck, you [strategic action] and [effect of the action].

- What were you telling yourself when you [successful action]?

- I saw how you [strategic action]. That made a huge difference!

- How did it help when you [strategic action]?

- Tell me one thing you did well today as a writer.

- I noticed how you [strategic action].

- Find your best descriptive sentence in this piece and read it for us.

- Tell me how you . . .

- You're thinking about experiences you've had. That will help you understand the characters' feelings.

- Show your table group what you just did and how it helped you.

- What do you notice?

- Keep going . . . You're on the right track!

- You're using the diagram so you can understand what the author's talking about.

- Why did you decide to [attempt]?

- I noticed that when you tried [attempt], you [effect].

- Did that work for you?

- I can tell that you [strategic action] because [effect]!

- You wanted to do [first attempt], but you tried [second attempt] and it worked!

- I noticed you had trouble with [problem] and then you fixed it and moved on. What happened in your head there?

- Did you see what just happened? You did [effort] and [effect]!

- What did you do that helped?

FEEDBACK THAT AFFIRMS

As students progress from talking about new behaviors to showing independence in them, our feedback can affirm their accomplishments. As you'll notice, affirming is essentially another way of naming students' successful behaviors (as previously discussed), and in fact, it can sometimes be difficult to pull the two apart. But there is a slight degree of difference.

When our feedback works to *name* student efforts, we generally do so to clarify and elaborate on emerging behaviors to build confidence and propel learners further across the zone of proximal development. *Affirming*, on the other hand, is more of an end-point response where we articulate successful behaviors in an effort to confirm and celebrate independence. Feedback that names helps students see what they're doing that's working, so they'll keep doing it, whereas feedback that affirms helps them reflect on their independence. Although both are about making students aware of their successful efforts so they'll become routine, one nudges, "You're getting there. Keep going!" and the other looks back on the journey and says, "Congratulations—you did it!"

When you affirm what your students are doing, remember to be specific with your praise. As discussed earlier, our feedback is far more constructive when we funnel our responses into process-driven comments that focus on effort and strategy. As you help children reflect on their work, what you celebrate together will get repeated, so make use of affirmative feedback to reinforce your students' efforts and applaud their success.

Examples of language that affirms:

- That's exactly what we've been talking about, and you did it perfectly!

- Are you proud of yourself? I can see why!

- You put a lot of thought into how your subtitles would help your readers stay on track.

- Go back through your reader's notebook and put a star on top of your three best entries.

- What a great workshop we had today! Everyone I conferred with today was ready to tell me what they needed help with when I got to them.

- You went back so you could check it! Good thinking!

- That's a different way to see it! Say it again, so everyone can hear it.

- You stopped reading when you got to the period.

- You're right! That big word is *interesting* . . . /In/ . . . /ter/ . . . /est/ . . . /ing/ . . . You got it!

- The descriptions you included in your writing helped me imagine your birthday party clearly.

- That's it! You're sitting up and taking charge of your book!

- You've learned to put spaces between your words . . . That makes it so much easier for us to read!

- Yep, that made sense and sounded right!

- That sounds just like how [character] would say it!

- These transition words like [*read a few out loud*] help move your story along from scene to scene.

- You figured it out all on your own! Smile for yourself.

- Good checking. You reread it so you could fix it.

- That [makes sense/looks right/sounds right].

- Your summary includes all the important elements of a biography. Way to go!

- That was a terrific example of what it should look like.

- When you read that part, it sounded just like talking!

- You put your finger on that word to figure it out and then pulled it back. And you did it all quickly!

- You figured out what was wrong and went back to fix it.

- Let's look back at your writing samples across the year and see how much you've grown.

- You're an expert at [strategy].

Understanding the vital role our feedback plays in the scaffolding process is an essential factor in moving our teaching to more effective levels and our learners to greater degrees of competence. The first step is to begin fine-tuning our language so that it builds on student strengths to reinforce our instruction. Seen individually, the types of constructive feedback discussed in this chapter—questioning, demonstrating, prompting, naming, and affirming—all have their own potential to influence that instruction. But in the end, these functions of language work best as they collectively highlight students' efforts and strategies in a useful, timely way. Considered together, their effects are exponential.

Responding to students well in the construction zone requires back-and-forth, split-second decision making as well as an understanding of the learner, our goals, and best instructional practices. Such an orchestration doesn't happen unintentionally, and you probably won't be working at game speed at first. You'll likely need to unlearn some old habits and form some new ones. Delivering constructive feedback takes practice. But more than that, it takes contemplation and good judgment along with a familiarity and an awareness of the ways in which our language contributes to our overall scaffolding attempts.

Here, we connect again to the intentional, reflective nature of scaffolding. Once we know where students are in light of where we're headed, we can craft more (or less) specific language with an eye toward effective instruction. In the next chapter, we'll revisit how the specificity of our language shifts across the gradual release progression, how it relates to our intentions, and the role all of this plays in helping learners ultimately take responsibility for their own learning.

CONSTRUCTIVE REFLECTIONS

1. Record (or have a peer write down) the feedback statements you make across one lesson, and then review your responses by sorting them into person-driven responses or process-driven responses. What do you notice, and how can this inform your future feedback practices?

2. Think about someone who encouraged you through a challenge. In what ways, both verbal and nonverbal, did they give you confidence? What effect did that have on your performance?

3. Think about some typical responses you use frequently, like "Thread it up" or "Get your mouth ready." How can you be certain that your students understand what you mean and know how to use your feedback to help themselves? Do any of your routine ways of responding need to be reconsidered?

4. Consider your usual wait time during instruction. Do you give learners enough time to absorb your feedback? What signs do you look for to ensure this? How can your practices around wait time contribute to the constructiveness of your responses?

5. How often do you ask generative questions in the scaffolding process? How can asking a question have a different effect from providing feedback as a direct response? Can you think of a situation where one might be more or less beneficial than the other?

6. The section "Feedback That Demonstrates" cautions us about being too explicit too often. What are the hidden dangers of this, have you seen them firsthand, and how do you determine when feedback that demonstrates is too explicit?

PART FOUR

RESPONSIBILITY

Our motivation in every scaffolding scenario is to place optimal levels of responsibility on the learner at every step in the process, so that our students are eventually independently responsible for the new knowledge.

CHAPTER 8 TEACHING FOR RESPONSIBILITY:
PUTTING LEARNERS IN CONTROL

When I was still a fairly new teacher, our grade level was given a distressing new directive. Instead of our traditional end-of-the-year assessment routines, we were told (in no uncertain terms) that we would no longer be administering our own final running records and comprehension surveys. Instead, we'd be trading with a peer to test their kids—and they in turn would test ours. Talk about ruffling some feathers! Amidst veiled cackles of rebellion, our entire henhouse marched to the office citing countless reasons why such an arrangement wouldn't work, along with insistent complaints about how unfair it was to our students.

But beneath our rumbling was something none of us really wanted to admit. The truth was that we were secretly afraid that when called on to read for another teacher, our students wouldn't do what we'd taught them to do—or at least wouldn't do it as well as they would for us. And we didn't like the odds.

In time, we came to see the real source of our resistance and were able to address it, but perhaps this experience resonates with you. If you've ever felt a pang of uncertainty at letting the instructional coach work with your kids, wondered desperately if your writers would pull through on an end-of-the-year assessment, or sat grading paper after paper and thinking to yourself, *I know I taught this, but you wouldn't be able to tell it from looking at these,* then you have a notion of what we were feeling.

As my teaching team owned up to our fears, we looked more closely at our instruction and realized that we'd been unintentionally grooming our students to depend on us for their success. As long as we were there to guide them, they were fine. But without us holding their hands and telling them what to do next, they faltered, and we struggled to see why. It wasn't pretty, but in time, we realized that we needed to get intentional about helping our students eventually do independently what they were able to do with our support. We became mindful of pushing them to higher levels of independence and stayed cautious about making them overly reliant on us.

If you find yourself in situations like this—where your learners can't seem to muster the same levels of success when you step away—the trouble might be that you haven't fully handed over the responsibility. The running record incident with my team opened my eyes to this critical stumbling block. Even if I was the best teacher in the world, how were my students ever going to perform on their own if I never stepped out of the picture? This happens a lot more than most of us like to admit. How often do we unintentionally leave our instructional scaffolds unfinished? How often do we metaphorically hold our students' hands for far too long in a nonstop pattern of support that never fully spurs them to self-sufficiency?

Even though this book has focused more specifically on our role as the more knowing other in the scaffolding process, don't forget: we aren't isolated participants here. The co-construction we do in the zone of proximal development is a shared effort, and children must understand that they have an important job in that process. But they can't assume the responsibility if we refuse to let them do so. We need to be mindful about this. As teachers, many of us have such an unconscious habit of grabbing the instructional reins that we often struggle to let someone else take over.

But take over is exactly what learners need to do. This is the essence of scaffolding. If we want students to eventually assume complete control, then we must orchestrate learning situations that constantly press them to practice optimal responsibility.

Scaffolding, though teacher guided, is student driven. In every instance of its instructional progression, what we do and say should trigger students to take on as much of the mental work as possible. This guiding principle drives scaffolding's fourth and crowning condition:

In every moment, effective scaffolds place optimal responsibility for learning on students as they move toward increasing degrees of independence.

If you look back on our previous common conditions, you'll notice that this has been a fundamental part of our discussions all along. That's because teaching for optimal responsibility is equally important for (1) keeping us *focused*, (2) alerting us of the need to be *flexible*, and (3) grounding what we say and how we say it as we give learners constructive *feedback*. Successful scaffolds empower students to become responsible, active participants in their learning. Without this essential thread, we may have a good idea of where we're going and maybe even some thoughts about what we might do and say to move things in that direction—but unless we stay intentional about who's primarily accountable (and what they're accountable for) along the way, our scaffolds can never fully take shape.

True scaffolding takes an in-depth knowledge of our children as well as the instructional practices that would best move them to independence. It involves a seamless, almost artlike dance to the beats of varying levels of support—a dance that is different for each learner and one where the steps can change based on the needs of the student and the focus of the instruction. As more knowing others, we take the lead in this dance, determined that our children will eventually move to the captivating melodies of reading and writing—all by themselves and without our guidance.

But we move cautiously. We know that leading too much will create readers who can't dance on their own or, worse, don't want to dance at all.

SHARING AND SHIFTING RESPONSIBILITY

It's a dangerous oversight to misinterpret scaffolding's finish line of full responsibility to mean that learners won't share some levels of responsibility along the way. Yes, ultimately, we want readers and writers to problem solve independently, without prompting or guidance from us. This is, after all, the goal. But that doesn't mean they'll wait until the end of the zone of proximal development to take ownership of their learning.

How do we know when our support is just right? How do we know when to offer help and when to pull back and allow children to take the lead and eventually go it alone? How much is too much, and for that matter, how little is too little?

As we answer these role-defining questions, it helps to flesh out a set of job descriptions (of sorts) that keep us mindful of exactly what we'll need to be doing and what we'll hold our students accountable for. To further refine these roles for yourself, look closely at Figure 8.1 and consider the ways in which responsibility progressively shifts across scaffolding and how these fluctuations are directly tied to student and teacher accountability. Notice how the level of responsibility we take while introducing a concept (showing) looks distinctly different from our teaching during the release of responsibility (sharing and supporting) and even more different as we encourage students' independence (sustain). And, while we're observing to see how things are going along the way (survey), we'll invite students to share varying degrees of responsibility in that process as well. As you transition from one instructional stage to the next, staying aware of this will help you mind the roles you'll share with students, so you can make sure they're working at optimal levels of responsibility.

In addition to insisting that we press students to do as much of the intellectual work as they're ready and able to do, teaching for optimal responsibility is about intentionally advancing the line. If we truly expect readers and writers to take over, then we have to start shifting our teaching in a way that purposefully passes the instructional baton. Staying mindful of the shared roles we play with students, we look for evidence that they are ready to take on increasing degrees of responsibility, create opportunities for them to do so, and mindfully support them in that process.

Being an effective kid watcher (survey) will play a key role in helping you decide when it's time to raise the bar and push students to take on more. Through formal and informal assessments, look closely at how your students are doing and consider their level of competence in relation to the instructional focus. As you do, think about whether their attempts show obvious strengths, highlight severe confusions, or reveal a need for some tweaking. I'm partial to the way Pat Johnson (2006) couches this. In *One Child at a Time*, she gives us a simple way to gauge this type of responsive teaching by asking ourselves if the instructional goal in question is one the student *can do*, *can almost do*, or *cannot do*.

	WHAT'S MY ROLE? (TEACHER RESPONSIBILITIES)	**WHAT'S MY STUDENT'S ROLE?** (STUDENT RESPONSIBILITIES)
Show	Largely in control, the more knowing other plans engaging instruction that explicitly defines, demonstrates, and explains a strategy, skill, or way of thinking while making clear how it can be useful to the learner.	Less in charge, but still active, the learner observes, listens, notices, and connects to the teacher's demonstration while reflecting on its significance and asking questions to clarify any misunderstandings.
Share	Here, the teacher creates opportunities that invite children into the work and begins carefully handing over responsibility—possibly giving feedback in the form of stronger, more specific prompts, nudges, or cues to assist learners while adjusting the scaffold as determined by their responses.	As students begin to take on some of the responsibility for the new learning, they attend to, consider, and respond to feedback while participating and "trying on" tentative knowledge and asking for assistance as needed.
Support	Continuing to hand over the responsibility, and doing so to a larger degree, the more knowing other allows students lots of time for practice while beginning to pull back, monitoring for the need to shore up confusions as necessary, and supporting learners with slight reminders and less explicit feedback.	At this stage, as learners become more and more accountable, they practice applying and orchestrating all they've learned with increasing levels of competence, seeking considerably less support as they internalize greater degrees of the learning.
Sustain	With the students either independent or well on their way, the teacher focuses on maintaining an environment that both creates and supports opportunities for learners to continue to apply newly mastered skills independently and in a variety of situations.	Now, more in control, learners build momentum from repeated successful efforts as they continue to practice and confidently use their new knowledge, strategies, and skills independently—without requiring much support from their more knowing other, if any at all.
Survey	Throughout the learning process, the teacher constantly monitors, observing and evaluating the students' processes and responses to instructional support and feedback, reflecting on this data, and adjusting the scaffold as needed.	From beginning to middle to end, learners (to the greatest extent possible) self-reflect and mind their own progress, noticing successful—and not so successful—attempts as they negotiate new areas of knowledge and move themselves toward increasing levels of independence.

Figure 8.1
Shared Responsibilities Across the Gradual Release Progression

Identifying these levels of student need showcases where we'll want to step in and support—and, just as important, where we'll need to step out. If we see that students *cannot do* it, a large part of the responsibility will fall on us as we offer higher levels of support. If, on the other hand, we establish that they *can almost do* it, we know we're in the middle of the gradual release progression where we'll be taking on more responsibility at first but intentionally pulling back as students get closer to independence. Finally, as we conclude that learners *can do* it, they're ready to take on full responsibility for the work as we offer reinforcements and we gradually remove our supports completely (see Figure 8.2).

As you look over these indicators plotted across the gradual release progression in Figures 8.1 and 8.2, it's critical to realize that the amount of support you'll give is directly proportional to the level of responsibility you're sharing with your student. As learners take more responsibility, your level of support will lower, but when they're less able to do so, they will understandably need more help from you.

In essence, what's considered *optimal responsibility* will shift as children progress across the zone of proximal development.

Cannot Do Independently	Can Almost Do Independently		Can Do Independently
TEACHER RESPONSIBILITY		STUDENT RESPONSIBILITY	
Show	Share	Support	Sustain

Figure 8.2
Locating Needs Across the Gradual Release of Responsibility Model

ON-THE-JOB TRAINING

As you identify scaffolding's shifting instructional roles, think twice before assuming kids will automatically know their responsibilities. One major task you have in handing over the reins is articulating for children exactly what they're being held accountable for, so they can clearly understand their function in the process. This might seem more obvious when you're asking students to do something brand new, but it's also important to remember (and easy to forget) when you're shifting things to a higher degree of responsibility on their part.

For an example, consider a modeled think-aloud. If your role in the think-aloud is to select the text, identify instructive examples, model your thinking, monitor student engagement, and read with emphasis phrasing and pacing that support comprehension, your students' role might be to listen attentively, watch for examples of thinking, and start reflecting along with you, perhaps noticing when their own thoughts resonate (or fail to resonate) with your examples. Though your students will certainly be carrying far less of the intellectual load in this instance, it's important to note that they do share *some* level of responsibility here.

With this in mind, just before your first session, you'll want to clarify the roles you and your students will play: "Readers, as I'm reading through this text, I'll stop and share my thinking with you. When I do, I want you to listen closely for two things: what I'm thinking and what in the book is making me think it. When I finish reading, I'm going to ask you to help me chart some of the things you noticed about my thinking, so be ready for that. Is everyone clear on what we're supposed to do?"

Later, as students prepare to take on more of the work, you'll want to spell out their shifting responsibilities, perhaps saying, "Readers, listen closely, because our jobs are about to change. The last few times we did a think-aloud, I did the thinking and we charted what you noticed about it afterward. Today as I'm reading, I'll stop and ask you to think. After you've had a few seconds to think, you'll share two things with your floor partner: what you're thinking and what from the book is making you think it. You'll have to be listening and thinking hard, because you never know when I'm going to stop. So . . . just to be clear, my job is to read, and your job is to think and share. Are we ready?"

In both instances, your instructions will help children see their responsibilities more clearly. If we want students to take an active role in their learning, we have to communicate what, exactly, that role is. Learners will generally do what we ask, but it's unfair to expect them to do something we haven't taken the time to clearly explain—so you'll want to be cautious about assuming they already know.

HELP WANTED . . .

Be cautious, as well, about any preconceived notions you might have about what your job is and what your students' job is. Though most of us do it unconsciously, it isn't unusual for us to hoard responsibilities that kids could readily take on if we'd only ask. Just as our earlier think-aloud example emphasized the often-forgotten but imperative responsibilities students have in the showing stages of the gradual release progression, children can play a vital role in many of the areas we might traditionally relegate entirely to teachers.

For example, take the role of assessment (survey). It had always been my practice to respond to a child's reading with the traditional "two glows and a grow." If you're unfamiliar with that phrase, it describes a process by which you bring readers back to the text and tell them two things they did well and then address something they struggled with.

A few years ago it dawned on me that this response, though well meaning, puts the responsibility for establishing areas of strength and weakness squarely on me. Don't get me wrong, there is definitely a time and a place for me to be the head surveyor, but it all comes down—again!—to intentionality. As the shared roles of responsibility shift forward through the gradual release progression, we have to shift who's validating strengths and who's identifying areas for growth.

These days, I still use two glows and a grow, but I'm far more mindful about it. Instead of jumping in after children read to tell them what they did well and where they could do better, I look for opportunities to hand the text to the reader and ask, "Can you show me a place where you did well?" and then, "Can you show me a place where you had trouble or would like some help?" What I've found remarkable is that when I allow students to guide these informal assessments, they're usually spot-on with what I was already thinking and sometimes even highlight areas for growth that take my scaffolds in entirely new directions.

Another area of responsibility we might be tempted to leave solely to the teacher is establishing an instructional focus. As the more knowing other, we often take the lead in choosing the goal for our scaffolds, but students can participate in this decision as well. In a way that is similar to how my perspective of two glows and a grow changed over time, I've come to understand that inviting students to be part of the goal-setting process can be a powerful way to increase ownership, and in doing so, raise motivation, engagement, and empowerment.

As a result, I now look for opportunities for students to tell me what they want to work on and where they'd like to improve. One way I keep this shared responsibility going is by kicking off most of my reading groups and reading conferences with the question "What are you working on right now as a reader?" When I went around the table in one of my recent first-grade groups, the answers ranged from "Holding my book and going fast" to "Using my finger when I'm stuck on a word" to "Checking the picture so it makes sense."

Children can often share more of the goal-setting responsibilities than we might be willing to let them. Whether they want to get through their first chapter book, pass their state writing test, or simply read a book to their grandma, young readers and writers have an innate desire to improve, and we can capitalize on that by making room for their instructional goals in our scaffolds. As you become more intentional about the instructional roles you share with students, be persistent about giving them responsibility—even in areas you might not typically think of, such as assessment and goal setting—and you'll soon notice your readers and writers taking more initiative.

SHIFTING SUPPORT

At some point we begin to let go so our learners can start to move on, and knowing when to hand over responsibility—not to mention how much and how quickly to hand it over—is directly tied to our ability to observe students (survey). Effective scaffolders are constantly monitoring learners and their responses for evidence that shows how much support they need, when they need it, and when students are ready for that assistance to be gradually removed and eventually taken away completely. At each turn, careful observations guide instructional decisions, ensuring that everything scaffolders do keeps their learners working at optimal levels of responsibility.

As you work with your own students, keep this in mind. Remember the importance of being a kid watcher and stay vigilant for signals that tell you your students are ready to take the next step. Though you'll continue to make your instructional decisions based on a variety of triangulated data, the deciding factor you'll want to home in on as you gear up to push students further is whether they're being successful at your current level of support. If they are, it's likely time to shift things forward.

For instance, say I'm working with a third grader to help him read with better phrasing, and I decide to model it while reading aloud from texts with embedded phrase boundaries. (For example, "The moon hung/ in the night sky.// As we waited for the fish to bite,/ I thought about Grandpa/ and how much we all missed him.//") As I do, I'll look for evidence that my demonstrations are resonating with him, and when I see that they are, I'll reduce my support by asking him to echo read behind each sentence I model. When, after several experiences with this level of support, I notice he's attending to the phrase boundaries with my example, he's ready to take on more.

Perhaps at first, I can encourage him to choral read along with me, but as soon as he shows me he can do this well, I'll be ready to pull back and let him do it alone. If he stalls a bit, I can jump in if needed, but for the most part, I want him on the job. When I see him consistently and effectively using phrase boundaries to read with appropriate phrasing, I'll remove the scaffold completely, perhaps reinforcing his success initially but eventually drawing back even that level of support.

Notice how every next step I take is directly preceded by an observation on my part. In that way, assessment guides our decisions to move students along the continuum of responsibility. When your collected evidence confirms your students' strengths at a particular level, increase your expectations and press them to take on more. The optimal level of responsibility advances like a moving target: as students graduate from one level of competence to the next, a new challenge emerges, shifting the entire teacher-support/student-responsibility paradigm further once again (see Figure 8.3).

A RETURN TO FLEXIBILITY: SHIFTING FORWARD

Neil Mercer (1995) emphasizes this flexible nature of shifting support, reminding us that the guidance we offer in the scaffolding process is "increased or withdrawn in response to the developing competence of the learner" (75). In other words, we fine-tune our instruction to meet the immediate needs of our students at each particular stage, considering where they were before and where we expect to take them next. As you take these forward-moving instructional steps, remember to constantly watch for firsthand evidence that tells you whether you're raising the bar too high, raising it too quickly, or dragging things along unnecessarily. Remember, as well, the importance of flexible instruction (see Chapter 5). If you're pulling back too much and notice your students start to slip, it makes perfect sense to double back, recalibrate, and offer additional support to shore things up. On the other hand, if evidence indicates that your students are ready for more independence earlier than you'd anticipated, be prepared to move with them while dialing your assistance back.

Each time you make evidence-based decisions to raise or lower your levels of support, you'll fluctuate between being *more involved* and *less intrusive*. As you think about how you'll move students to take on increasing amounts of responsibility, consider how you'll adjust your actions along the range of teacher involvement. In the same way that I'd gradually change my involvement from explicit assistance to less direct supports as my third-grade reader learns to read with phrasing, every action you take in the scaffolding

TEACHER RESPONSIBILITY

STUDENT RESPONSIBILITY

SHIFT: The teacher removes the phrase boundaries completely, so the student can practice reading with appropriate phrasing without them.

EVIDENCE: With effortless automaticity, the reader uses phrase boundaries to read with appropriate phrasing.

SHIFT: The teacher discontinues reading and encourages the student to do the work for himself while she monitors to make sure the current level of support is appropriate and reinforces as needed.

EVIDENCE: The reader's competence grows during the choral reading, and his confidence increases.

SHIFT: The teacher invites the reader to join in by choral reading with her in the same manner.

EVIDENCE: The reader consistently mimics his teacher's demonstrations of phrasing with phrase boundaries.

SHIFT: The teacher continues to model phrasing using phrase boundaries, but invites the reader to echo her example by rereading with similar phrasing and cadence behind her.

EVIDENCE: The reader grasps the purpose of phrasing and phrase boundaries while attending to his teacher's modeling.

SHIFT: The teacher models appropriate phrasing using phrase boundaries while explicitly describing how this supports fluency and meaning.

EVIDENCE: When reading, the student reads with a monotone word-by-word cadence and phrasing.

As the student reaches mastery, the scaffold shifts again to address a new level of need, and the entire process begins again.

Figure 8.3
Shifting Responsibility Based on Observational Evidence

process should shift to correlate directly with the optimal level of responsibility you want children to aspire to. Here are a few examples:

> **Shifting Your Timing**—As you transition from higher to lower levels of support, your response time may shift from fairly immediate prompting when students are learning a new skill to progressively delayed reminders as students improve and need you to jump in less frequently. For instance, when a student requiring a lot of support struggles, you'll want to quickly direct him with helpful responses. However, as this same student grows into his abilities, you'll probably want to give him some time to call up what he knows before offering assistance.

> **Shifting Your Scaffolds (n.)**—You'll also want to gradually reduce your visual, auditory, and physical scaffolds. For instance, say you start out working with students using large anchor charts that you frequently review together. As children show a need for less guidance, you might transition to table tents, and later move on to less obvious bookmark reminders. In another example, you could start off singing the "Letters Start at the Top" song as you practice letter formation, but as students progress, just hum it when a writer goes to start a letter and forgets. Physical scaffolds should gradually fall off as well. As they develop greater degrees of competence, readers no longer need their finger to match their voice to print, and writers move away from using a craft stick to hold the space between their words as they write.

> **Shifting Your Physical Presence**—There's a reason we bring students close to us for shared reading and interactive writing and want them even closer for guided reading lessons. When students are first learning a new skill or strategy, proximity matters. Initially, you'll pull up alongside them

and work closely, often with your hand over theirs.
But as soon as they start to take over, you'll want
to sit back and take your hands out of the page. As
students become more self-sufficient, you might
switch to roaming nearby as you monitor their
progress, circling back to offer assistance only
when needed.

Through it all, we remember that scaffolds are temporary. As we make important decisions that urge learners toward greater self-reliance across the zone of proximal development, our supports fade into the background while our readers and writers gradually take control and we become less and less involved.

A RETURN TO FEEDBACK: SHIFTING OUR LANGUAGE

Your responses to students will follow a pattern of fading teacher support as well. In Chapters 6 and 7, we looked at the effects of our feedback and discussed the power behind what we say and how we say it to constructively move learners forward. As we continue to look at releasing responsibility, we'll build on those earlier discussions, highlighting how the language we choose parallels the increasing degrees of responsibility we're scaffolding students toward. For instance, consider the difference between the following statements we might say to a young reader:

"Watch how I use the picture when I'm stuck on a word."

"You looked at the picture, and that helped you figure out that hard word!"

Both are effective forms of instructional feedback, but which one associates the majority of the responsibility with the teacher and which one places it on the student? Which response would best serve a reader who's just learning to search the picture for story meaning, and which would support a student who's already doing this well? Each of these statements can serve an empowering purpose at different points across the scaffolding continuum, but the more we consider them, the more we confirm that one response doesn't fit every need. Effective feedback correlates directly with where we are in the various stages of the gradual release progression. And in the same way a plumber uses the right tool for the job, we have to be intentional about using the right language to move readers and writers ahead.

Just as we shift instructional actions for this purpose, we can change the words we say and the intention behind them to advance learners from modeling to sharing to independence. Even small adjustments in how we say things can make a big difference. Figure 8.4 shows the way in which several sets of language shift across the continuum of release. As you review it, take a moment to notice a few things. First, as we move from left to right across the continuum, our language typically progresses from more involved to less intrusive. For example, the transition from "Watch me do it" to "Let's do it together" to "You try it" to "You did it!" verbally traces a gradual evolution from high teacher support to high student responsibility.

Notice, as well, how our language in the scaffolding process advances from explicit explanations to direct prompts, eventually moving on to general reminders and cues as students gain control before finally finishing with responses that affirm their independent processing. To encourage movement across the continuum of gradual release, we can adjust our responses to help students leapfrog forward in their learning, matching each stage with its particular type of language support:

Show—direct, explicit language that demonstrates a model, inviting learners to attend to and notice how it's done and how it can help them improve. This interaction may call students' attention to something the teacher is demonstrating or something other effective readers and writers do.

> "Watch how I do this. Before I try to write the word,
> I say it out loud a few times slowly to stretch it
> out. When I do, I'm listening for all its sounds and
> thinking about the parts I know."

> "Let's look at some examples of the way Eve
> Bunting uses dialogue to show us what her
> characters are feeling."

Share—specific language that begins to hand over responsibility by inviting learners to step into the work, encouraging them to start attempting what they can't yet do alone, and supporting them through their first tentative attempts and approximations.

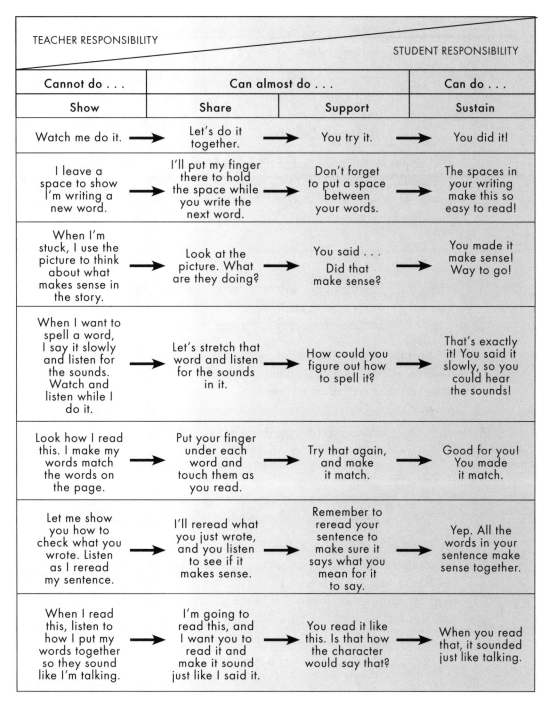

Figure 8.4
Feedback Across the Gradual Release Progression

> "Now let's do it together. Let's stretch that word and listen for the parts we know."

> "Try this. Instead of writing that your brother was mad when you lost his cell phone, you could write out what he was saying to you—you know, like Eve Bunting did. I'll help."

Support—language that reminds students of something they've perhaps forgotten or prompts them to do something the teacher is certain they know how to do. Here, the feedback is far more general than showing and sharing, pushing a greater degree of the thinking onto the student.

> "Remember . . . Say it slowly."

> "In the part where your mom gets upset that you and your brother are fighting, how could you show your readers how angry she was?"

Sustain—less intrusive language that encourages, notices, and affirms students' effective attempts so they'll repeat successful efforts and continue to grow into their competence.

> "I saw you stretch that word so you could hear its parts! Smile for yourself!"

> "When you wrote how your little sister stands up and yells for everyone to stop arguing, I could really tell how tired she was of everyone fighting."

Survey—language that identifies strengths and weaknesses, either through observational comments, clarifying questions, or noticing the successful (or not-so-successful) effects of the student's efforts. The responsibility for pinpointing these areas may fall to the teacher or the student, depending on the situation.

> "Show me how you stretched it, and let's see if I can help."

"Read what you wrote again. How does that sound
to you? Does what he's saying make you feel how
angry he was?"

As we work to move students closer to independence, our language,
too, must transition forward, encouraging them toward the optimal levels of
responsibilities they'll take on next. When we craft our feedback in a way that
gradually reduces our involvement, our students step up and become more
accountable. In this way, our speech patterns can empower readers and writers
to take an active role in the learning process.

Shift your language, and you'll shift the responsibility!

IT'S ALL ABOUT "YOU"!

One thing you might have noticed in Figure 8.4 is where the word *you*
appears compared with its pronoun counterparts *I* and *we*. Pronouns are strong
indicators of responsibility, and as you become more intentional about your
feedback language, you'll want to ensure that everything you say is mirroring
your intention to shift learning forward.

Think about the words *you*, *I*, and *we,* and notice how they change across the
gradual release progression in Figure 8.4. Marriage counselors the world over
caution couples about how these words imply different levels of culpability.
For instance consider the difference between *"*You make me so angry when
you spend all evening at your mother's!" and its slightly different take, "I get
angry when you spend all evening at your mother's." Certainly, the root issue's
the same, but the responsibility for the anger shifts—if only slightly—from
the first statement to the second, creating a different reality. One makes you
responsible for my mood, whereas the other holds me accountable for it.

In a more academic example, sentences such as "I put a period here,"
"Listen to how I read it," or "When I read a poem, I make a picture in my
mind" would fall to the left of the gradual release continuum, which might
be fine if that's where you are in the scaffolding process. But what if you're
near the middle? What if you're near the end? Sentences such as "Watch me
while *I* do it" indicate that I am the one largely in control of the situation,
whereas statements such as *"We* can summarize this article by thinking about
the important information and the order in which it was presented" imply a
shared role between our students and us. But with responses such as "What
from the text makes *you* say that?" we send a message that the student is
accountable for the thinking.

As you read over the following example, think about how the teacher's language—and, more specifically, the use of the pronoun *you*—helps focus optimal responsibility on the student:

Reader:

[*reading*] The pig is asleep in the . . . [*puts finger over the letter* h *and then stalls*]

Teacher:

You seem stuck. What are *you* telling *yourself* there?

Reader:

[*shows the letters* ay] I know these . . . It says /ay/. But . . . [*looks up*]

Teacher:

You found a part *you* know, but *you* aren't sure what to do next.

Reader:

[*scrunches face*] Yeah.

Teacher:

Is there another part *you* know?

Reader:

[*points to the letter* h] I think . . . Like in *hat* [*looks for letter sound chart*]?

Teacher:

So, *you've* seen it before. How could that help *you*?

Reader:

Um . . . /h/ . . . /h/ . . . /ay/ . . . hay. The pig is asleep in the hay!

Teacher:

Were *you* right?

Reader:

No?

Teacher:

Well, what else could *you* check?

Reader:

[*looks at picture*] Hay! It is hay! /h/ . . . /ay/ The pig is asleep in the hay.

Teacher:

Were *you* right this time?

Reader:

Yes!

Teacher:

How do *you* know?

Reader:

I checked the picture and used the letters!

Teacher:

Good for *you*! *You* used the picture to think about the story and thought about the parts of the words *you* know to figure it all out. Smile for *yourself*!

This isn't an exact science, and you don't have to get hypervigilant about it, but it is worth considering how this small shift in our language can affect the positions of responsibility in our scaffolds. For more examples, take a look at the list of responses in Figure 8.5, and notice how the word *you* implies accountability, moving the work away from the teacher and closer to the student. If your goal is for students to take on increasing levels of independence, stay mindful of the pronouns you use as you respond to them. Shifting from *I* to *We* to *You* is another way we can adjust our feedback to reflect the forward-moving responsibility of our scaffolds.

- How could *you* help *yourself?*
- What could *you* try?
- How do *you* know?
- What else could *you* check?
- Where could *you* look for help?
- Think about what *you* already know that could help *you*.
- Show *yourself* the hard part.
- Do *you* see a part *you* already know?
- Do *you* notice anything that could help?
- *You* figured it out all by *yourself!*
- *You* tried to do it on your own before asking for help.
- What are *you* working on as a reader?
- What were *you* thinking when *you* worked through that?
- What makes *you* say that?
- Here's something *you* could try . . .
- *You're* ready for a writer's secret . . .
- Were *you* right?
- *You* must be proud of *yourself!*
- How did *you* use the text to help *yourself?*
- What could *you* check?
- *You* said . . . Does that make sense/sound right/look right?
- How does that help *you* as a reader?
- What keeps *you* from using a capital there?
- What did *you* do well?
- What other things were *you* trying in your head to figure that out?
- Smile for *yourself. You* worked hard!

Figure 8.5

Placing Responsibility on *You*

Moving young readers and writers toward optimal levels of responsibility means we gradually step back and fade out while encouraging our learners to step up and take charge. This isn't a chance happening. Rather, it's deliberate, decisive, and above all, intentional.

When we teach in the construction zone, we make sure that at every stage, in every moment, our instructional decisions lead students to do as much of the work as they can and, when they're ready, press them to take on more. As our readers and writers rise to these challenges, we remove our instructional supports completely and release them to ultimate independence.

Balancing these levels of teacher support and student challenge may not be easy at first, but you'll get the hang of it. "You'll know when and how to release more responsibility to students as you learn what they need from them," literacy specialist Debbie Miller assures. "So, put yourself in the moment, teach, and listen to what your students have to say. You don't have to know everything, but you do know something. Be genuine. Listen. Be open to new ideas and ways of thinking. And when you are, you'll know in your heart and mind what comes next. You really will" (2011).

All you have to do is create a constructive environment for your students; orchestrate instructional interactions that invite them to become active, responsible participants in their learning; and then get out of their way and let them.

But one question still remains: are you getting in the way?

Let's find out . . .

CONSTRUCTIVE REFLECTIONS

1. If you were to ask your students, "What is your job in the learning process?" how do you think they would respond? How would their answers vary between your more advanced learners and your struggling learners? Would these hypothetical answers change the way you look at your instruction? Or would they affirm your current practices?

2. How do you identify and monitor for optimal levels of responsibility in your scaffolds? Do you struggle to find the appropriate level of student accountability? What are some signs you could watch out for that would help you know when your supports are just right, too much, or not enough?

3. Think about an area of responsibility you have difficulty sharing with your students. What keeps you from handing it over? And how might releasing it more readily affect the outcomes of your instruction?

4. This chapter identifies students' current level of success as a major determinant of when it's time to adjust your scaffolds and urge learners forward. What other evidence do you take into account when you're ready to make this decision?

5. How mindful are you of the instructional shifts in your feedback? Are there certain responses you use habitually at every level of the scaffolding process? How could you change your language to fall more in line with the levels of responsibility you want your children to assume?

6. Can you think of situations in your personal life where your unconscious use of pronouns has sent a hidden message of responsibility? Has your awareness around this changed? If so, what ramifications can such a realization have on the conversations you have with your students? What instructional adjustments might you make as a result?

CHAPTER 9   MONITORING FOR RESPONSIBILITY:
KNOWING WHEN TO LET GO

Keeping your readers and writers working at their highest levels of independence is a critical part of working in the construction zone, and pulling this off successfully takes an enormous amount of intentional preparation and ongoing reflection on your part. You work hard to identify your focus. You prepare flexible instruction to address that focus. You anticipate the constructive feedback you'll likely give students, and you keep a cautious eye out for shifting responsibility to move learners forward. This is definitely hard work. And, the very last thing you'd expect—after all this effort—is to find out that *you're* the one impeding your students' progress.

But sometimes, despite our best intentions, this is exactly what happens. As we round out our discussion of scaffolding and, more specifically, the role students working at optimal levels of responsibility plays in that process, we take a final, introspective look at our own practices and ask

Am I getting in the way?

This question challenges us to look for and identify any unconscious habits we may have that keep the ball of responsibility in our court. Essentially, it asks, "In spite of everything, are my attempts to move learners forward actually holding them back?" Asking ourselves whether we're unintentionally doing something to obstruct the very process we're trying to facilitate can be one of the most difficult questions we ask as more knowing others, because doing so involves critical levels of self-reflection.

And we may not always like what we see.

WHEN TOO MUCH IS TOO MUCH: OVERSCAFFOLDING

When I set out to write this book, I knew we'd need to address some areas where our scaffolds frequently fall short and, more specifically, common teaching interactions where we might not be providing enough support. To that end, we've reviewed the pitfalls of unfocused and inflexible scaffolds along with the importance of constructive feedback and responsive teacher language. With each of these conversations we've built a collective case for offering just-right amounts of teacher support in our scaffolds. But to paint a complete picture, we'll need to finish things up by shifting our focus from addressing insufficient levels of assistance to scenarios where the exact opposite is true— situations where, rather than provide too little support, we provide too much.

We close, then, with a caution about overscaffolding: a condition where we offer excessive supports or fail to remove our supports over time, keeping readers and writers from engaging in the learning process at optimal levels of responsibility and leading us to do much of the work they could do on their own.

I'm sure many of us can admit to times when we overscaffolded without even realizing it. It's an incredibly easy thing to do—especially if we don't know to look out for it. That's why staying aware of ways we might be helping too much is an important first step. Being mindful of our own teaching behaviors helps us monitor for instances where our overscaffolding gets in the way so we can put an end to those patterns that hold learners back.

In its simplest form, overscaffolding occurs when the supports we originally put in place to help learners never get taken away. Remember, we build scaffolds knowing they'll eventually be dismantled. But if we don't have a plan for removal, we run the risk of making our readers and writers dependent on assistance they no longer need and that can even hinder their progress.

Think about how the instructional supports mentioned in the following examples might actually get in the way of student independence and optimal responsibility:

- Requiring **graphic organizers** to plan nonfiction summaries despite evidence that students no longer need them to summarize effectively.

- Asking students to continue **finger pointing** after they're able to track print fluently with their eyes.

- Leaving **anchor charts** up that have long since served their purpose.

- Using "What to do when you're stuck on a word" **prompting cards** even after readers are effectively using most of the strategies illustrated.

- Giving long, drawn-out **book introductions** in guided reading that leave nothing new for the group to discover and work through on their own.

- Assigning an excessive number of **writing prompts** that keep writers from finding and developing meaningful topics by themselves.

- Continuing to **model** or **share** activities that students are ready to try on their own.

Each of these scenarios includes supports that, though certainly valuable at one time, are no longer necessary. When they've lingered too long past their prime, scaffolds (such as finger pointing and graphic organizers) can actually slow down students' progress and may even frustrate them, reducing their motivation and engagement. Even using particular forms of feedback too often can get in the way, especially when doing so interrupts your students' flow of thought and ability to process independently. Use caution and be mindful of the types of assistance you leave in place too long and how doing so might affect the levels of responsibility your students are encouraged to take on. When our supports become perpetual habits rather than temporary scaffolds, we rob learners of valuable opportunities to experience the confidence that comes from taking on increasingly difficult challenges on their own and succeeding.

RESCUING: SCAFFOLDING'S EVIL TWIN BROTHER

Recently, I had a chance to work for several weeks with a group of teachers who were eager to take a good, strong look at their teaching practices. I asked them to identify four students for daily, individual tutoring just after school let out for the summer. In addition to coaching them during their individual tutoring sessions, I offered to design an ongoing staff development program to support them and their instructional goals. During the planning stages, the teachers asked that we spend time investigating their use of language to support their students' movement to independence.

To that end, I asked them to record their lessons and transcribe them for the group. During our staff development time each day, one of the teachers would share a transcript of a lesson, and we would look at the way she used language to encourage readers to higher levels of competence.

As we investigated their instruction, I began to notice a recurring pattern. The group seemed to have a desperate need for their students to do well. And, why wouldn't they? Isn't that the crux of a powerful guided reading lesson: to cater our book introductions and our scaffolds in such a way that the reading— and the reader, as a result—is successful? But it seemed to run deeper than that. They definitely had a sense of urgency for their readers to *get it right*. However, the problem was that many of their students didn't seem to share that same sense of urgency. The teachers were working harder than their readers were. And, in some instances, they were doing almost all the work.

This sent up a red flag, and I decided we needed to take a closer look at the intentions behind their instructional decisions. As we reviewed their lesson transcripts, we noticed an overall pattern of teaching that included an impulsive need to sweep in and help at the slightest moment of difficulty. Sound familiar?

When I asked the group to share their assumptions about this pattern, some initially reasoned that they were working within the zone of proximal development, some wondered if maybe they were jumping in too soon, and a few admitted that they really weren't sure why they were teaching this way.

We revisited the gradual release progression, and I asked them to think about where they were on the scale of support during those moments. After lots of conversation about what it means to scaffold instruction, we realized that when our scaffolds aren't strong and our students start to falter as a result, we tend to grab at straws instructionally—desperately trying whatever we can to "save the lesson." We wanted our readers to feel successful, but at the moment they weren't. Fear and uncertainty had us jumping in (often too soon), taking over, and carrying the weight of the work.

Eventually, we came to recognize this behavior as *rescuing* and dedicated the rest of our staff development time to investigating how rescuing occurs, how to differentiate it from scaffolding, and how we can adjust our instructional techniques to prevent it. Rescuing, we determined in the end, is another form of overscaffolding. And even though it's far less obvious than leaving supports in place for too long, it can be just as detrimental: instructional rescuing demonstrates an impeding behavior where the more knowing other assumes full responsibility for the learning effort, losing sight of the learner's level of responsibility entirely.

WHEN RESCUING ISN'T HELPING

There is a fine line between scaffolding and rescuing, and in many ways, their similarities can be confusing. It's an easy mistake, because when you think about it, both rescuing and scaffolding stem from a foundation of collaboration and assistance. Both are helping behaviors. Both scenarios denote a more capable person (teacher) supporting a needier individual (learner).

Despite these connections, rescuing and scaffolding often play polar opposites of each other (see Figure 9.1). In our work, we learned to differentiate the two by reflecting on one overarching concept: responsibility. I often ask teachers, "Who do you think worked harder during that lesson—you or the student?" In a rescuing situation, the teacher is generally the only one working—the sole responsibility is placed on the rescuer. On the other hand, when the instructional plan honors optimal levels of responsibility, the student is working just as hard as the more knowing other, if not harder, as the teacher assumes a facilitative role—supporting, modeling, and encouraging, but *not* taking over the reader's work. In essence, scaffolding dictates a shared responsibility with a goal in mind. Effective scaffolders offer just the right amount of support to make it easy to learn.

Rescuers simply take over.

THE RESCUED

Whether consciously or unconsciously, rescuers envision learners as helpless—people who can't do it on their own or are simply unable to pull themselves out of whatever got them bogged down in the first place. Although it can happen with just about any student in any situation, it appears to occur most often when working with struggling learners, reluctant learners, English language learners, and any of our "harder to teach" students. Since many teachers don't want to risk pushing these readers and writers even further away, they may feel reluctant or uncertain as they urge them toward optimal levels of responsibility.

SCAFFOLDING	RESCUING
Planned —We have a specific idea of where the instruction is going and stick to it.	**Unprepared**—We're not sure exactly where we're going with the lesson, but we're hoping for the best.
Easy to learn—We dig our heels into the ZPD, supporting learners in just the right way so they feel safe taking risks when things are challenging.	**Easy to give up**—Our teaching behaviors encourage learners to abandon their attempts, sit back, and let someone else do it.
Intentional—Every move we make is exact, decided, and well reasoned.	**Chance**—We're grabbing at straws and unsure of whether our teaching moves are appropriate.
Proactive—We anticipate student behaviors and needs as we prepare our lessons.	**Reactive**—Our teaching decisions are knee-jerk at best, often leaving us unsure of their effectiveness.
Derived from knowledge—We make sound decisions based on what we know about the learner and best instructional practices.	**Arrives from discomfort and uncertainty**—We aren't sure what to do, so our dissonance prompts us to jump in without reflecting.
Assumes innate ability—We know our learner has the strength inside to take on the task at hand as we wait, trust, and facilitate.	**Assumes helplessness**—Perhaps unconsciously, we may not trust learners to step up and may be unsure whether they can be successful without us.
Deliberate—We plan ahead, stay focused, and fill our bag of tricks with appropriate, intentional teaching moves derived from our own professional development.	**Accidental**—Our instructional moves can be rash and hit or miss, and although we may score some terrific teaching moments, we aren't always sure why or how they occurred.
Calculated—Our lessons and conversations are tightly focused, and we don't lose sight of the goal.	**Impulsive**—The lesson is loose and hurried, leaving our teaching feeling vague and scattered.
Student focused—Every move we make is dependent on the student taking some level of responsibility, and we strive to promote strategies students will use when working independently.	**Instructor focused**—We've taken so much responsibility that when we step out of the situation, the learning stops or reverts to its previous status.
Plan for removal—We understand that all scaffolds are built to be removed eventually, and we move forward with that goal in mind.	**No plan for removal**—Our instructional language and supports are the same for most of our lessons, making them inadvertently stagnate.
Intentionally shared workload—We understand that scaffolding takes two and are mindful of the dual responsibilities of the learner and the teacher.	**Teacher doing most of the work**—In an effort to move the lesson along, we control the conversation and the text while the student lets us.
Empowering—Both learner and teacher walk away from the lesson feeling valued and capable—a natural by-product of true reciprocal learning.	**Exhausting**—Both learner and teacher are tired from the instructional push and pull and overall disconnect of the lesson.
Expects active readers and writers—We address apathy in our teaching as well as our learners and insist that they sit up, participate, and "take the bull by the horns."	**Generates passive readers and writers**—We allow learners to take part as quasi-involved participants, unintentionally training them to do the same when it comes time to work independently.

Figure 9.1
Are You Scaffolding or Rescuing?

Since many of these children come to us with a sense of learned helplessness—a pervasive feeling of apathy that comes from hitting one too many instructional brick walls—both teacher and student seem primed for a rescue scenario to unfold. This is unfortunate, as these are exactly the students who need our intentionally scaffolded focus the most. Because of this, instructional rescuing is often ironically counterproductive. In a classic case of best intentions, our readers and writers grow accustomed to our rescuing behaviors and learn that if they wait long enough, someone will eventually feel sorry for them and jump in to do the work for them.

Keep a special eye out for learners like this who've grown so comfortable with being rescued that they're more than happy to let someone else take over. If instructional rescuing courts passive readers and writers under the fog of learned helplessness, we can combat that pattern by cultivating a stronger sense of agency. Johnston (2004) describes a sense of agency as a feeling that "if [students] act, and act strategically, they can accomplish their goals" (29). In other words, we want learners to become active participants in the learning process and take part in their own growth. We want them to understand that they can change their world and that their actions can affect their learning. But that means our instruction must invite them to rise to the challenge.

THE RESCUERS

Last year, a second-grade teacher asked if I could help her sort some things out about one of her students. As we reviewed the notes she kept on her lessons, I noticed an unfamiliar code—*T helped*—showing up frequently in her comments. Curious, I asked her what it meant. "Oh," she replied, "that just means that he was having a hard time, so I helped him out: you know, gave him some pointers so he could get unstuck."

"Okay," I said. "Do you do that a lot?"

She shuffled through several sets of her notes, considering. "Yeah, it looks like I do. Is that wrong?"

"What do you think?" I asked.

"Well, I mean . . . probably so. Especially if I really want to see what he can do without my help. You know?"

"Yeah, that makes sense." I thought out loud, "But what I'm really wondering is—what would happen *if you didn't help so much*?"

A few days later, I met up with her in the teachers' lounge. I could tell by her smile that she'd figured it out. "Oh my gosh, Terry!" she exclaimed. "I'm so glad I learned that about myself. I can't believe I was doing it! I want to tell everyone." She went on to tell me that as she stepped back more, she noticed that the student in question wasn't having near as much trouble as she'd originally presumed. "I asked him if he likes it when I help less, and he said that he does because it gives him time to think. It turns out, my jumping in wasn't helping him as much as I thought."

Teachers are essentially helpers, and any one of us might don our rescuing cape at different times. It comes with the territory. But it's one of those traits where less is more. And although I agree that some teachers are chronic rescuers, rescuing isn't a full-time sport for most of us. It really is about looking at our own instruction and simply reflecting on our tendencies.

Some teachers tend to rescue more with needier readers, whereas others might rescue more when their overall energy is low or they're having a bad day. We may rescue when we're uncomfortable with a particular area of instruction or haven't planned our lessons as well as we'd like. Some teachers rescue randomly based on the perceived needs of students in a particular instructional moment, and still others rescue out of a need to feel effective.

Rescuing appears to happen most when we don't have a strong plan for the scaffold in place or when we skip a step in the scaffolding process. And of course it would: when we've left learners high and dry without any support system, it feels like they need rescuing. For example, I've noticed a common situation where we're left to feel like we have no choice but to rescue—and it's one we often set ourselves up for.

By now, you're familiar with the fundamental gradual release progression that shifts from modeling to sharing to independence. When navigated correctly, this process (show, share, support, sustain, survey) delivers solid results. But when we neglect steps in this process, we create a situation ripe for rescuing behaviors. For instance, if we model a skill but then skip immediately to expecting independence, we've overlooked the critical sharing component. The same thing can happen when we move immediately to sharing or independence without first clearly demonstrating what we expect children to do. These oversights are generally unintentional, and teachers are often unaware they even happened. But consider how they create incomplete and unstable scaffolds that set our readers and writers up to eventually need someone to sweep in and catch all the falling pieces.

IS YOUR RESCUING GETTING IN THE WAY?

To help you root out possible rescuing behaviors in your own instruction, use the following reflective questions to consider how you interact with your students. If you answer yes to more than just a few, it may be time to take a closer look at your teaching patterns.

Do you often find the momentum of your lesson waning without a good reason?

Although there are plenty of other variables that may be at the root of this problem, rescuing is one you might consider. It isn't unusual for a rescuer's lesson to start out with a bang and then fizzle out. I've noticed that this problem is twofold: the teacher tires from "dragging the student along," and the learner tires from the boredom of having to sit through it.

Do you find yourself physically holding the text, turning the pages, pointing to difficult parts as your learners sit back, physically uninvolved?

Although there are certainly times when these teaching behaviors are necessary, they are fewer than most of us would like to think. Rescuers have difficulty pulling themselves away from the table and letting students give it a try on their own. If you notice this in your own teaching, consider doing a pushback experiment, where you remove yourself physically from the learning by sitting back with your hands in your lap as you listen in on your readers or writers. For many of us, this is surprisingly difficult, but it can tell you a lot about your tendencies to help students at times when it may not be necessary.

Are you exhausted after a lesson?

If you're anything like most of the teachers I work with, this could be true simply because we work so hard. I mean, most of us walk around exhausted! But in this case, the fatigue in question has a different source. As a result of taking on most of the responsibility around the learning, teachers who rescue often work harder than their students, leaving themselves utterly exhausted, despite having started out fairly energized.

Are you doing most of the talking?

Rescuers tend to take over the conversations in their teaching—often to the point of answering their own questions—so the learner doesn't have to. Talking too much can be a sign that you're doing the majority of the work. Monitor who's doing most of the talking as you teach. If it's you, it's highly likely that your students aren't taking optimal levels of responsibility during your lessons.

Do you avoid challenging students for fear of where that challenge might take you?

As a defense mechanism, rescuers often want the lesson to flow smoothly, so they avoid sticky situations at all costs. They plan unchallenging lessons. They ask low-level questions. And they especially tend to steer clear of ambiguous situations where they can't control the outcome. In this way, they're preemptive—avoiding scenarios in which the learner would need to be rescued at all.

Is it difficult for you to allow students to work through a hard part on their own? Could your wait time use a bit more time?

Many rescuers jump in entirely too soon. And when they do, they generally take on the work themselves. If too much time has gone by, consider jump-starting the stall with a decisive, well-placed prompt such as "I see you're stuck there. What could you do to help yourself?"

Do you struggle to take notes on student reading or writing behaviors?

Though not always indicative of a rescuer, it might be that you can't take good instructional notes because you're too busy doing the learner's work for him or her and your hands are all over the text. With a slight adjustment to include taking notes, this is another great place to consider a pushback experiment.

Do you generally ask closed questions?

As we've discussed previously, closed questions usually require a one-word answer without a lot of thinking. (For example, "Did the character solve her problem?" versus "What can you tell me about how the character tried to fix the problem?") This is a common form of rescuing, mainly because closed questions give the illusion that both the teacher and the student are successful. For tickles and grins, a friend and I once challenged ourselves to teach for ten minutes without using a closed question. We both lasted about two and had a good laugh at how difficult this really is! Certainly, teaching with 100 percent open questions is near impossible (and likely not productive), but simply striving for more open conversations than closed will have positive effects on your interactions with learners.

Do you dodgeball your students with follow-up questions without allowing them to really share their thinking?
This is a frequent rescuer behavior. Many of us risk an open-ended question only to follow it up all too quickly with an onslaught of closed questions out of our discomfort with the silence students' thinking time invokes. When a fourth-grade teacher I worked with realized he was doing this, he immediately put a stop to it. Later he told me he was blown away by the effect it had on his students, saying, "They've all benefited from having more time to discuss and process, especially my strugglers."

Do you struggle to define a focal point for your lesson, teach many lessons on the fly, or have difficulty keeping your lesson focused?
Even though it may all seem important, we can't teach everything at once. Staying focused supports instruction that is more deliberate in its scaffolding. Without a focus, our lessons can feel scattered, leaving us feeling unprepared. And when we're unprepared, we tend to rescue more.

You'll want to note that, on their own, none of these behaviors is an immediate indicator of rescuing. And certainly, the reflections listed make allowances for the countless other issues you deal with at any given moment in your classrooms. Nevertheless, these questions can be a good self-assessment tool to help you stay mindful as you gauge your instruction and work to identify rescuing behaviors that need some fine-tuning.

Deliberately planned and intentionally executed scaffolding is the antithesis of overscaffolding and instructional rescuing. It takes intentional planning on our part, not to mention lots of practice, but the first step is awareness. When we take the time to monitor our instruction, keeping an eye out for ways we might be getting in the way of optimal responsibility, we take a powerful step toward helping our students become independent, lifelong learners.

Anything we do that keeps us from releasing responsibility to our learners does them a disservice, and it can be especially problematic when our overscaffolding gives us the illusion that we're helping. Any time we do what kids could do on their own; any time we say what they could say; any time we jump in to rescue them, offer too much support, or leave those supports in place for far too long, we diminish our scaffolding efforts and keep our young readers and writers from reaching their full potential.

Even if we think we're helping.

In the end, what looks simple and spontaneous on the outside is the result of extreme intention on our part—observing, noticing, and reflecting—throughout the entire scaffolding process as we make necessary adjustments to nudge our children toward increasing degrees of competence and press them to optimal levels of responsibility.

This is what teaching in the construction zone is all about.

For learners to eventually reach independence, they'll need lots of experiences with us where they're encouraged to take the lead. Early one morning, Jason stopped by my classroom to return a book. Like I usually did, I asked him if he had a few minutes to read with me. "Sure," he said, shrugging. He pulled out a chair at my small-group table.

As he sat down to read, I thought about how far Jason had come. By now, we both knew the routine. He'd show up about once a week under the guise of dropping off a book, and I'd ask him to read with me before he left. That was it. Jason *wanted* to read with me, but it was still best if it was my idea. I had to ask.

I was okay with this arrangement. It was a far cry from just a few months before, when getting Jason to read anything was a near impossibility. But it was more than that. Everything about him seemed different. He was reading with more confidence and was eager to show what he knew. He was monitoring and self-correcting and becoming faster and more efficient as the year progressed. I was excited for him and wanted to encourage him to keep it up.

"Jason, as I was listening to you just now, I was thinking about you as a reader and noticing how much better you're doing," I said as I put our things away. "You're taking charge and pushing through the hard parts, and you sound much smoother when you read. You're not the reader you used to be. I was wondering if maybe you could tell me what's different."

"Well, Mr. Thompson," he said in all seriousness, "I've been teaching myself how to read."

As he bounded off to class, I thought about his response. The claim itself—*I've been teaching myself how to read*—was simple enough, but it spoke volumes. In his own way, Jason was making a profound statement about his role in the learning process.

From the moment we begin working with young learners, our task is to hand over responsibility in a way that puts them in control to the greatest extent they can be. Even as we guide the process, our instructional moves should send a clear message to readers and writers that although we're here to help, this is unquestionably their job. To Jason's way of thinking, this meant he was in charge of teaching himself to read, and my role—quite frankly—was to support him in that process.

This is how it should be.

When done well, scaffolding in the construction zone creates a safe place where just-right levels of affective and academic support empower young readers and writers to independently meet challenges they never could before. It's a place where strengths are acknowledged, potential is released, and confidence becomes a shelter from self-doubt. A place where everything looks right and sounds right, and it all finally makes sense.

And, it's also a place where—if you listen hard enough—you'll hear the soft, encouraging voice of a more knowing other saying, "Go on . . . You can do this now. You don't need my help anymore."

CONSTRUCTIVE REFLECTIONS

1.   What are some unconscious things you do that tend to get in the way of your students' progression toward independence? How has your awareness about your own instructional practices around this concept changed?

2.   Think about various lessons you've taught in your time as a teacher. Can you identify situations where you've left certain supports in place too long? What effect did this have on your scaffolds and your learners' levels of responsibility?

3. Who do you tend to rescue most often? What type of learner causes you to sweep in and take over? How can being mindful of this shift your responses with these particular students?

4. What is your reaction to learners who've grown so accustomed to being rescued that they passively sit by, waiting for you to take on the majority of the work? How do you address this with them? How do you address it with yourself?

5. When are you most likely to rescue? In which situations do you find yourself inadvertently helping too much? How can knowing this about yourself affect your scaffolding efforts?

6. Which of the ten reflective questions listed in the last section of this chapter resonated with you the most and why? What steps will you take as a result of those reflections?

7. As you finish this chapter—and in doing so, come to the end of this book—what are *your* constructive reflections? What are you going to do differently or more mindfully when you go to school tomorrow?

REFERENCES

Appelt, Kathi. 2008. *The Underneath*. New York: Simon and Schuster.

Berk, Laura E., and Adam Winsler. 1995. *Scaffolding Children's Learning: Vygotsky and Early Childhood Education*. Washington, DC: National Association for the Education of Young Children.

Clay, Marie. 2005. *Literacy Lessons: Designed for Individuals: Part Two: Teaching Procedures*. Portsmouth, NH: Heinemann.

Daniels, Harvey. 2002. *Literature Circles: Voice and Choice in Book Clubs and Reading Circles*. 2nd ed. Portland, ME: Stenhouse.

Day, Nicholas. 2012. "Down with Training Wheels." *Slate*, May 11. http://www.slate.com/articles/life/ family/2012/05/training_wheels_don_t_work_balance_bikes_teach_children_how_to_ride_.2.html.

Dorn, Linda J., and Tammy Jones. 2012. *Apprenticeship in Literacy: Transitions Across Reading and Writing, K–4*. 2nd ed. Portland, ME: Stenhouse.

Duke, Nell K. 2011. "Helping Students Learn to Read and Write Informational and Procedural Text: Five Principles for Instruction at Any Grade Level." Presentation to the Alamo Reading Council, San Antonio, TX, September.

Dweck, Carol. 2006. *Mindset: The New Psychology of Success*. New York: Random House.

Fisher, Douglas, and Nancy Frey. 2012. "Close Reading in Elementary Schools." *The Reading Teacher* 66 (3): 179–188.

Ginsburg, Herbert P., and Sylvia Opper. 1988. *Piaget's Theory of Intellectual Development*. 3rd ed. Englewood Cliffs, NJ: Prentice Hall.

Goetz, Thomas. 2011. "Harnessing the Power of Feedback Loops." *Wired*, July. http://www.wired. com/2011/06/ff_feedbackloop/.

Harris, Theodore L., and Richard E. Hodges, eds. 1995. *The Literacy Dictionary: The Vocabulary of Reading and Writing*. Newark, DE: International Reading Association.

Jensen, Eric. 2009. *Teaching with Poverty in Mind: What Being Poor Does to Kids' Brains and What Schools Can Do About It*. Alexandria, VA: Association for Supervision and Curriculum Development.

Johnson, Pat. 2006. *One Child at a Time: Making the Most of Your Time with Struggling Readers, K–6*. Portland, ME: Stenhouse.

Johnston, Peter H. 2004. *Choice Words: How Our Language Affects Children's Learning*. Portland, ME: Stenhouse.

———. 2012. *Opening Minds: Using Language to Change Lives*. Portland, ME: Stenhouse.

Kamins, Melissa L., and Carol Dweck. 1999. "Person Versus Process Praise and Criticism: Implications for Contingent Self-Worth and Coping." *Developmental Psychology* 35 (3): 835–847.

Koenig, Rhoda. 2010. *Learning for Keeps: Teaching the Strategies Essential for Creating Independent Learners*. Alexandria, VA: Association for Supervision and Curriculum Development.

Landrigan, Clare, and Tammy Mulligan. 2013. *Assessment in Perspective: Focusing on the Reader Behind the Numbers*. Portland, ME: Stenhouse.

Martinelli, Marjorie, and Kristine Mraz. 2012. *Smarter Charts: Optimizing an Instructional Staple to Create Independent Readers and Writers*. Portsmouth, NH: Heinemann.

Marzano, Robert J., Debra J. Pickering, and Jane E. Pollock. 2001. *Classroom Instruction That Works: Research-Based Strategies for Increasing Student Achievement*. Alexandria, VA: Association for Supervision and Curriculum Development.

Medina, John. 2008. *Brain Rules: 12 Principles for Surviving and Thriving at Work, Home and School*. Seattle, WA: Pear Press.

Mercer, Neil. 1995. *The Guided Construction of Knowledge: Talk Among Teachers and Learners*. Tonawanda, NY: Mutilingual Matters.

Mercer, Neil, and Steve Hodgkinson, eds. 2008. *Exploring Talk in School*. Thousand Oaks, CA: SAGE.

Miller, Debbie. 2011. "Releasing Responsibility." *ChoiceLiteracy.com*, August. https://www.choiceliteracy.com/articles-detail-view.php?id=311.

———. 2013. *Reading with Meaning: Teaching Comprehension in the Primary Grades*. 2nd ed. Portland, ME: Stenhouse.

Pearson, P. David., and Margaret C. Gallagher. 1983. "The Instruction of Reading Comprehension." *Contemporary Educational Psychology* 63 (5): 317–344.

Pink, Daniel H. 2009. *Drive: The Surprising Truth About What Motivates Us*. New York: Riverhead.

Routman, Regie. 2008. *Teaching Essentials: Expecting the Most and Getting the Best from Every Learner, K–8*. Portsmouth, NH: Heinemann.

———. 2011. "Highly Effective Teaching, Coaching, and Leading: Essential Practices That Accelerate Reading and Writing Achievement, Engagement, and Enjoyment." Presentation to the Georgia Conference on Teaching Reading and Writing, Perry, GA, June.

Rutherford, Paula. 2012. *Instruction for All Students*. 2nd ed. Alexandria, VA: Just ASK Publications and Professional Development.

Sousa, David A. 2011. *How the Brain Learns*. 4th ed. Thousand Oaks, CA: Corwin.

Stiggins, Rick, Judith Arter, Jan Chappuis, and Steve Chappuis. 2004. *Classroom Assessment for Student Learning: Doing It Right—Using It Well.* Portland, OR: Assessment Training Institute.

Thompson, Terry. 2010. "Are You Scaffolding or Rescuing?" ChoiceLiteracy.com, January. https://www.choiceliteracy.com/articles-detail-view.php?id=735.

Wood, David, Jerome Bruner, and Gail Ross. 1976. "The Role of Tutoring in Problem-Solving." *Journal of Child Psychology and Psychiatry* 17 (2): 89–100.

Vygotsky, Lev S. 1978. *Mind in Society: The Development of Higher Psychological Process*. Ed. and trans. Michael Cole, Vera John-Steiner, Sylvia Scribner, and Ellen Souberman. Cambridge, MA: Harvard University Press.

———. 1986. *Thought and Language*. Ed. and trans. Alex Kozulin. Cambridge, MA: MIT Press.

INDEX